Amadeus

A DRAMA

by

Peter Shaffer

SAMUEL FRENCH, INC.
45 WEST 25TH STREET   NEW YORK 10010
7623 SUNSET BOULEVARD   HOLLYWOOD 90046
LONDON   *TORONTO*

BILLING AND CREDIT REQUIREMENTS

All producers of AMADEUS must give credit to the Author in all programs and in all instances in which the title of the Play appears for purposes of advertising, publicizing or otherwise exploiting the Play and/or production. The author's name *must* appear on a separate line in which no other name appears, immediately following the title of the play, and *must* appear in size of type not less than fifty percent the size of title type.

Opening night December 17, 1980.

BROADHURST THEATER

Ⓢ A Shubert Organization Theatre

Gerald Schoenfeld, *Chairman*   Bernard B. Jacobs, *President*

THE SHUBERT ORGANIZATION
ELIZABETH I. McCANN   NELLE NUGENT
ROGER S. BERLIND

present

IAN McKELLEN
TIM CURRY   JANE SEYMOUR

in

AMADEUS

by

PETER SHAFFER

with

| GORDON GOULD | PATRICK HINES | NICHOLAS KEPROS |
| JONATHAN MOORE | LOUIS TURENNE | EDWARD ZANG |

Production Designed by
JOHN BURY

Associate Scenic Designer   *Associate Costume Designer*   *Associate Lighting Designer*
URSULA BELDEN   **JOHN DAVID RIDGE**   **BEVERLY EMMONS**

Music Directed and Arranged by
HARRISON BIRTWISTLE

Directed by

PETER HALL

The world premiere of AMADEUS was given in London
by the National Theatre of Great Britain.

The Producers and Theatre Management are Members
of The League of New York Theatres and Producers, Inc.

4

CAST

(*in order of appearance*)

ANTONIO SALIERI . . . . *Ian McKellen*

THE "VENTICELLI" . . . . *Gordon Gould,*
Edward Zang

SALIERI'S VALET . . . . *Victor Griffin*

SALIERI'S COOK . . . . *Haskell Gordon*

JOSEPH II, EMPEROR OF AUSTRIA . . . . . . *Nicholas Kepros*

JOHANN KILIAN VON STRACK . . . . *Jonathan Moore*

COUNT ORSINI-ROSENBERG . . . . *Patrick Hines*

BARON VAN SWIETEN . . . . *Louis Turenne*

PRIEST . . . . *Donald C. Moore*

GIUSEPPE BONNO . . . . *Russell Gold*

TERESA SALIERI, WIFE OF SALIERI. . . . . . . *Linda Robbins*

KATHERINA CAVALIERI, SALIERI'S PUPIL . *Caris Corfman*

CONSTANZE WEBER, WIFE OF MOZART . . . *Jane Seymour*

WOLFGANG AMADEUS MOZART. . . . . *Tim Curry*

MAJOR DOMO. . . . . *Philip Pleasants*

CITIZENS OF VIENNA . . . . *Caris Corfman, Michelle Farr,*
Russell Gold, Haskell Gordon,
Victor Griffin, Donald C. Moore,
Brad O'Hare, John Pankow,
Philip Pleasants, Linda Robbins

VALETS. . . . . *Ronald Bagden, David Bryant,*
Rick Hamilton, Richard Jay-Alexander,
Peter Kingsley, Mark Torres

The action of the play takes place in Vienna
in November 1823, and, in recall, the decade 1781-1791.

THERE WILL BE ONE INTERMISSION

STANDBYS AND UNDERSTUDIES

Standbys and understudies never substitute for listed players unless
specific notification is made at the time of the performance.

Standby for Ian McKellen — Daniel Davis

Understudy for Mozart — John Pankow; for Constanze — Caris Corfman; for Joseph II, "Venticello" and Giuseppe Bono — Philip Pleasants; for von Strack, van Swieten and Salieri's Valet — Russell Gold; for Orsini-Rosenberg and Salieri's Cook — Donald C. Moore; for "Venticello" — Rick Hamilton; for Teresa Salieri and Katherina Cavalieri — Michele Farr; for Major Domo and Valets — Brad O'Hare; Second Mozart Understudy — David Bryant.

The first production of AMADEUS was given in London by the National Theatre of Great Britain on the 2nd November, 1979. It was directed by Peter Hall, designed by John Bury, and music realized by Harrison Birtwistle.

6

THE *'s which now and then divide the page indicate changes of Scene: but there is to be no interruption. The scenes must flow into one another without pause from the beginning to the end of the play.

P.S.

NOTE:

The words and lines enclosed in square brackets ([ ]) have been cut from the New York production.

CHARACTERS

ANTONIO SALIERI

WOLFGANG AMADEUS MOZART

CONSTANZE WEBER, *wife to Mozart*

JOSEPH II, *Emperor of Austria*

COUNT JOHANN KILIAN VON STRACK, *Groom of the Imperial Chamber*

COUNT FRANZ ORSINI-ROSENBERG, *Director of the Imperial Opera*

BARON GOTTFRIED VAN SWIETEN, *Prefect of the Imperial Library*

TWO 'VENTICELLI', 'LITTLE WINDS': *purveyors of information, gossip and rumour.*

MAJOR DOMO

SALIERI'S VALET. *(Silent part)*

SALIERI'S COOK. *(Silent part)*

TERESA SALIERI, *wife of Salieri. (Silent part)*

KATHERINA CAVALIERI, *Salieri's pupil. (Silent part)*

GIUSEPPE BONNO. *(Silent part)*

CITIZENS OF VIENNA

The VENTICELLI also play the TWO GALLANTS at the party in ACT ONE.

The CITIZENS of VIENNA also play the SERVANTS who move furniture and bring on props as required, and TERESA SALIERI and KATHERINA CAVALIERI, neither of whom have any lines to speak.

The action of the play takes place in Vienna in November 1823, and in recall, the decade 1781-1791.

THE SET

Amadeus can and should be played in a variety of settings. What is described in this text is to a large extent based on the exquisite formulation found for the play by the designer John Bury, helped into being by the director, Peter Hall. I was of course in enthusiastic agreement with this formulation, and set it down here as a tribute to admirable work.

The set consisted basically of a handsome rectangle of patterned wood, its longest sides leading away from the viewer, set into a stage of ice-blue plastic. This surface shifted beguilingly under various lights played upon it, to show gunmetal grey, or azure, or emerald green, and reflected the actors standing upon it. The entire design was undeniably modern, yet it suggested without self-consciousness the age of the Rococo. Costumes and objects were sumptuously of the period, and should always be so wherever the play is produced.

The rectangle largely represented interiors: especially those of Salieri's salon; Mozart's last apartment; assorted reception rooms, and opera houses. At the back stood a grand proscenium sporting gilded cherubs blowing huge trumpets, and supporting grand curtains of sky-blue, which could rise and part to reveal an enclosed space almost the width of the area downstage. Into this space superb backdrops were flown, and superb projections thrown, to show the scarlet boxes of theatres, or a vast wall of gold mirrors with an immense golden fireplace, representing the encrusted Royal Palace. In it also appeared silhouettes of scandal-mongering citizens of Vienna, or the formal figures of the Emperor Joseph II of Austria and his brocaded courtiers. This wonderful upstage space, which was in effect an immense Rococo peep show, will be referred to throughout this text as the Light Box.

***

On stage, before the lights are lowered in the theater, four objects are to be seen by the audience. To the left, on the wooden rectangle, stands a small table, bearing a cake-stand. In the center, further upstage and also on the wood, stands a wheelchair of the eighteenth century, with its back to us. To the right, on the reflecting plastic, stands a beautiful forte-piano in a marquetry case. Above the stage is suspended a large chandelier showing many globes of opaque glass.

All directions will be given from the viewpoint of the audience.

Changes of time and place are indicated throughout by changes of light.

In reading the text it must be remembered that the action is wholly continuous. Its fluidity is ensured by the use of servants played by actors in eighteenth-century livery, whose role it is to move the furniture and carry on props with ease and correctness, while the action proceeds around them. Through a pleasant paradox of theater their constant coming and going, bearing tables, chairs or cloaks, should render them virtually invisible, and certainly unremarkable. This will aid the play to be acted throughout in its proper manner; with the sprung line, gracefulness and energy for which Mozart is so especially celebrated.

Amadeus

ACT ONE

SCENE I

PLACE: *Vienna.*

TIME: *Darkness.*

*Savage whispers fill the theatre. We can distinguish
    nothing at first from this snake-like hissing save
    the word SALIERI! repeated here, there and
    everywhere around the theatre. Also, the word
    ASSASSIN!*

*The whispers overlap and increase in volume, slashing
    the air with wicked intensity. Then the light grows
    U. to reveal the silhouettes of* MEN *and* WOMEN
    *dressed in the top hats and skirts of early nineteenth
    century—* CITIZENS OF VIENNA, *all crowded together
    in the Light Box, and uttering their scandal.*

WHISPERERS. *Salieri! . . . Salieri! . . . Salieri!* (D. *in
the wheelchair with his back to us, sits an* OLD MAN. *We
can just see, as the light grows a little brighter, the top
of his head encased in an old cap, and perhaps the shawl
wrapped around his shoulders.*) *Salieri! . . . Salieri!
. . . Salieri!* (TWO MIDDLE-AGED GENTLEMEN *hurry in
from either side, also wearing the long cloaks and tall
hats of the period. These are the* TWO VENTICELLI:
*purveyors of fact, rumour and gossip throughout the
play. They speak rapidly—in this first appearance extremely rapidly—so that the scene has the air of a fast
and dreadful Overture. Sometimes they speak to each*

*other; sometimes to us — but always with the urgency of
men who have ever been first with the news.*)

VENTICELLO 1. I don't believe it.
VENTICELLO 2. I don't believe it.
VENTICELLO 1. I don't believe it.
VENTICELLO 2. I don't believe it.
WHISPERERS. *Salieri!*

VENTICELLO 1. They say.
VENTICELLO 2. I hear.
VENTICELLO 1. I hear.
VENTICELLO 2. They say.
VENTICELLO 1 & VENTICELLO 2. *I don't believe it!*
WHISPERERS. *Salieri!*

VENTICELLO 1. The whole City is talking.
VENTICELLO 2. You hear it all over.
VENTICELLO 1. The cafes.
VENTICELLO 2. The Opera.
VENTICELLO 1. The Prater.
VENTICELLO 2. The gutter.
VENTICELLO 1. They say even Metternich repeats it.
VENTICELLO 2. They say even Beethoven, his old pupil.
VENTICELLO 1. But why now?
VENTICELLO 2. After so long?
VENTICELLO 1. Thirty-two years!
VENTICELLO 1 & VENTICELLO 2. *I don't believe it!*
WHISPERERS. SALIERI!

VENTICELLO 1. They say he shouts it out all day!
VENTICELLO 2. I hear he cries it out all night!
VENTICELLO 1. Stays in his apartments.
VENTICELLO 2. Never goes out.
VENTICELLO 1. Not for a year now.
VENTICELLO 2. Longer. Longer.
VENTICELLO 1. Must be seventy.

VENTICELLO 2. Older. Older.

VENTICELLO 1. Antonio Salieri—

VENTICELLO 2. The famous musician—

VENTICELLO 1. Shouting it aloud!

VENTICELLO 2. Crying it aloud!

VENTICELLO 1. Impossible.

VENTICELLO 2. Incredible.

VENTICELLO 1. I don't believe it!

VENTICELLO 2. I don't believe it!

WHISPERERS. SALIERI!

VENTICELLO 1. I know who *started* the tale!

VENTICELLO 2. *I* know who started the tale! (*Two old men—one thin and dry, one very fat—walk on from either side: Salieri's* VALET *and* PASTRY COOK.)

VENTICELLO 1. (*Indicating him.*) The old man's Valet!

VENTICELLO 2. (*Indicating him.*) The old man's Cook!

VENTICELLO 1. The Valet hears him shouting!

VENTICELLO 2. The Cook hears him crying!

VENTICELLO 1. What a story!

VENTICELLO 2. What a scandal! (*The* VENTICELLI *move quickly* U., *one on either side, and each collects a silent informant.* VENTICELLO ONE *walks down eagerly with the* VALET; VENTICELLO TWO *walks down eagerly with the* COOK.)

VENTICELLO 1. (*To* VALET.) What does he say, your Master?

VENTICELLO 2. (*To* COOK.) What does he cry, the Kapellmeister?

VENTICELLO 1. Alone in his house—

VENTICELLO 2. All day and all night—

VENTICELLO 1. What sins does he shout?

VENTICELLO 2. The old fellow—

VENTICELLO 1. The recluse—

VENTICELLO 2. What horrors have you heard?

VENTICELLO 1 & VENTICELLO 2. *Tell us! Tell us! Tell us*

at once! What does he cry? What does he cry? What does he cry? (VALET *and* COOK *gesture towards* SALIERI.)

SALIERI. (*In a great cry.*) MOZART!!! (*Silence.*)

VENTICELLO 1. (*Whispering.*) Mozart!

VENTICELLO 2. (*Whispering.*) Mozart!

SALIERI. *Perdonami, Mozart! Il tuo assassino ti chiede perdono!*

VENTICELLO 1. (*In disbelief.*) Pardon, Mozart!

VENTICELLO 2. (*In disbelief.*) Pardon your Assassin!

VENTICELLO 1 & VENTICELLO 2. *God preserve us!*

SALIERI. *Pietà, Mozart. Mozart pietà!*

VENTICELLO 1. Mercy, Mozart!

VENTICELLO 2. Mozart, have mercy!

VENTICELLO 1. He speaks in Italian when excited!

VENTICELLO 2. German when not!

VENTICELLO 1. *Perdonami, Mozart!*

VENTICELLO 2. Pardon your Assassin! (*The* VALET *and the* COOK *walk to either side of the stage, and stand still.* Pause. *The* VENTICELLI *cross themselves, deeply shocked.*)

VENTICELLO 1. There was talk once before, you know.

VENTICELLO 2. Thirty-two years ago.

VENTICELLO 1. When Mozart was dying.

VENTICELLO 2. He claimed he'd been poisoned.

VENTICELLO 1. Some said he accused a man.

VENTICELLO 2. Some said that man was Salieri.

VENTICELLO 1. But no one believed it.

VENTICELLO 2. They *knew* what he died of!

VENTICELLO 1. Syphillis, surely.

VENTICELLO 2. Like everybody else. (*Pause.*)

VENTICELLO 1. (*Slyly.*) But what if Mozart was right?

VENTICELLO 2. If he really *was* murdered?

VENTICELLO 1. And by him. Our First Kapellmeister!

VENTICELLO 2. Antonio Salieri!

VENTICELLO 1. It can't possibly be true.

VENTICELLO 2. It's not actually credible.

VENTICELLO 1. Because *Why?*

VENTICELLO 2. Because Why?

VENTICELLO 1 & VENTICELLO 2. *Why on earth would he do it?*

VENTICELLO 1. And why confess *now?*

VENTICELLO 2. After thirty-two years!

WHISPERERS. SALIERI!

SALIERI. *Mozart! Mozart! Perdonami! . . . Il tuo assassino ti chiede perdono! (Pause. They look at him—then at each other.)*

VENTICELLO 1. What do you think?

VENTICELLO 2. What do you think?

VENTICELLO 1. I don't believe it!

VENTICELLO 2. *I* don't believe it!

VENTICELLO 1. All the same . . .

VENTICELLO 2. Is it just possible? . . .

VENTICELLO 1 & VENTICELLO 2. (*Whispering.*) *Did he do it after all?!*

WHISPERERS. SALIERI! (*The* VENTICELLI *go off. The* VALET *and the* COOK *remain, on either side of the stage.* SALIERI *swivels his wheelchair around and stares at us. We see a man of seventy in an old stained dressing-robe, shawled. He rises and squints at the Audience as if trying to see it.*)

* * * *

SALIERI'S Apartments.
November 1823. The small hours of the morning.

SALIERI. (*Calling to Audience.*) Vi Saluto! Ombri del Futuro! Antonio Salieri—a vostro servizio! (*A clock outside in the street strikes three.*) I can almost see you in your ranks—waiting for your turn to live. Ghosts of the Future! Be visible. I beg you. Be visible. Come to this dusty old room—this time, the smallest hours of dark November, eighteen hundred and twenty-three—and be my Confessors! Will you not enter this place and stay with me till dawn? Just till dawn—till six o'clock! . . . Did you hear them? Vienna is a City of Slander. Everyone tells tales here: even my servants. I keep only two now—(*He indicates them.*) —they've been with me ever since I came here, fifty years ago. The keeper of the Razor: the Maker of the Cakes. One keeps me tidy, the other keeps me full. (*To them.*) "Leave me, both of you! Tonight I do not go to bed at all!" (*They react in surprise.*) "Return here tomorrow morning at six precisely—to shave, to feed, your capricious master!" (*He smiles at them both and claps his hands in gentle dismissal.*) Via. Via, via, via! Grazie! (*They bow, bewildered, and leave the stage.*) How surprised they are! . . . They'll be even more surprised tomorrow: Indeed they will! (*He peers hard at the Audience, trying to see it.*) Oh, won't you appear? I need you—desperately! This is now the last night of my life. Those about to die implore you! What must I do to make you visible? To raise you up in the flesh to be my last, last audience? . . . Does it take an Invocation? That's how it's always done in Opera! Ah yes, of course: that's it. An *Invocation.* The only way. (*He rises.*) Let me try to conjure you *now*—Ghosts of the distant Future—so I can see you. (*He gets out of the wheelchair and huddles over to the fortepiano. He stands at the instrument and begins to sing in a high cracked voice, interrupting himself at the end of each sentence with figurations on the keyboard in the manner of a Recitativo Secco. During this the House Lights slowly come up to illuminate the Audience.*) •

(*Singing.*)

Ghosts of the Future!

Shades of Time to come!

So much more unavoidable than those of
    Time gone by!

Appear with what sympathy Incarnation
    may endow you!

Appear you —

The yet-to-be-born!

The yet-to-hate!

The yet-to-*kill!*

Appear — Posterity!

(*The light on the Audience reaches its maximum. It stays like this during all of the following.*)

(*Speaking again.*) There. It worked. I can see you! That is the result of proper training. I was taught invocation by Chevalier Gluck, who was a true Master at it. He had to be. In his day that is what people went to the Opera for: the raising of God and Ghosts . . . Nowadays, since Rossini became the rage, they prefer to watch the antics of hairdressers. (*Pause.*) Scusate. Invocation is an exhausting business! I need refreshment. (*He goes to the cake-stand.*) It's a little repellent, I admit — but actually the first sin I have to confess to you is Gluttony. Sticky gluttony at that. Infantine — Italian gluttony! The truth is that all my life I have never been able to conquer a lust for the sweetmeats of Northern Italy where I was born. From the ages of three to seventy-three my entire career has been conducted to the taste of almonds sprinkled with sifted sugar. (*Lustfully.*) Milanese biscuits! Sienna macaroons! Snow dumplings with pistachio sauce! . . . Do not judge me too harshly for this. All men harbour patriotic feelings of some kind. . . . [Of course I was born in 1750, when no man of sophistication would have dreamed of talking about Love of Country, or Native Earth. We were men of Europe, and that was enough.] My parents were Italian subjects of the Austrian Empire, a small town merchant and his small town wife. Their notion of Place was the tiny town of Legnago—which I could not wait to leave. Their notion of God was a superior Hapsburg Emperor inhabiting a Heaven only slightly further off than Vienna. All they asked of God was to keep them forever unnoticed—preserved in mediocrity. My own requirements were very different. (*Pause.*) I wanted Fame. Not to deceive you. I wanted to *blaze*, like a comet, across the firmament of Europe. Yet only in one especial way. Music. Absolute music! A note of music is either right or wrong—*absolutely!* Not even Time can alter that: music is God's art. (*Excited by the recollection.*) Already when I was ten a spray of sounded notes would make me dizzy almost to falling! By twelve, my one desire was to join all the composers who had celebrated God's glory through the long Italian past! . . . Every Sunday I saw Him in Church, painted on the flaking wall. [I don't mean Christ. The Christs of Lombardy are simpering sillies with lambkins on their sleeves. No: I mean] An old candle-smoked God in a mulberry robe, staring at the world with dealer's eyes. Tradesmen had put him up there. Those eyes made bargains, real and irreversible. "You give me so—I'll give you so! No more. No less!" (*He eats a sweet biscuit in his excitement.*) One night I went to see Him—and made a bargain with Him myself! I was a sober sixteen, filled with a desperate sense of right. I knelt before the God of Bargains, and I prayed [through the mouldering plaster] with all my soul. (*He kneels. The lights in the Audience go out slowly.*)

SALIERI. "Signore, let me be a Composer! Grant me sufficient Fame to enjoy it. In return I will live with virtue. I will be chaste. I will strive to better the lot of my fellows. And I will honour You with much music all the days of my life!" As I said Amen, I saw his eyes flare. (*As "God".*) "Bene. Go forth Antonio. Serve Me and Mankind—and you will be blessed!" . . . "Grazie!" I called back. "I am Your Servant for life!" (*He gets to his feet again.*) The very next day, a family friend suddenly appeared—out of the blue—took me off to Vienna and paid for me to study music! (*Pause.*) Shortly afterwards I met the Emperor of Austria, who favoured me—and was to advance my career beyond all expectations! *Clearly my bargain had been accepted! (Pause.)* The same year I left Italy, a young prodigy was touring Europe. A miraculous virtuoso aged ten years. Wolfgang Amadeus Mozart. (*Pause. He smiles at the Audience.*) (*Pause.*) And now—Gracious Ladies! Obliging Gentlemen! I present to you—for one performance only—my last composition, entitled *The Death of Mozart,* or *Did I Do it?* . . . dedicated to Posterity on this—the last night of my life! (*He bows deeply, undoing as he does so the buttons of his old dressing-robe. When he straightens himself—divesting himself of this drab outer garment and his cap—he is a young man in the prime of life, wearing a sky-blue coat and the elegant decent clothes of a successful composer of the seventeen-eighties.*)

* * * *

Transformation to the Eighteenth Century.

*Music sounds softly in the background: a serene piece
for strings by Salieri.* SERVANTS *enter. One takes
away the dressing-robe and shawl; another places
on the table a wig-stand bearing a powdered wig — a
third brings on a chair and places it at the* L.,U.

At the back the blue curtains rise and part to show the
EMPEROR JOSEPH II *and his* COURT *bathed in golden
light, against a golden background of mirrors and
an immense golden fireplace. His Majesty is seated,
holding a rolled paper, listening to the music. Also
listening are* COUNT VON STRACK; COUNT ORSINI-
ROSENBERG; BARON VAN SWIETEN; *and an anony-
mous* PRIEST *dressed in a soutane. An old wigged*
COURTIER *enters and takes his place at the keyboard:* KAPELLMEISTER BONO. SALIERI *takes his wig
from the stand.*

SALIERI. (*In a young man's voice: vigorous and confident.*) The place throughout is Vienna. The year — to
begin with — 1781. [The age still that of the Enlightenment: that clear time before the guillotine fell in France
and cut all our lives in half.] I am thirty-one. Already a
prolific composer to the Austrian Court. I own a respectable house and a respectable wife — Teresa. (*Enter*
TERESA: *a padded placid lady who seats herself uprightly
in the* U. *chair.*) I do not mock her, I assure you. I required only one quality in a domestic companion — lack
of fire. And in that omission Teresa was conspicuous.
(*Ceremoniously he puts on his powdered wig.*) I also
had a prize pupil: Katherina Cavalieri. (KATHERINA
*swirls on from the opposite side: a beautiful girl of
twenty. The music becomes vocal: faintly, we hear a*
SOPRANO *singing a concert aria. Like* TERESA'S,
KATHERINA'S *part is mute — but as she enters she stands*

by the forte-piano, she energetically mimes her raptur-ous singing. At the keyboard old Bonno *accompanies her appreciatively.*) Later to become the best singer of her age, she was a bubbling student with merry eyes and a sweet, eatable mouth. I was very much in love with Katherina — or at least in lust. But because of my vow to God, [I was entirely faithful to my wife.] I had never laid a finger upon the girl — except occasionally to de-press her diaphragm in the way of teaching her to sing. My ambition burned with an unquenchable flame! Its chief goal was the post of First Royal Kapellmeister, then held by Giuseppe Bonno — (*indicating him.*) — seventy years old, and apparently immortal. (*All on stage, save* Salieri, *suddenly freeze. He speaks very directly to the Audience.*) You, when you come, will be told that we musicians of the Eighteenth Century were no better than servants: the willing slaves of the well-to-do. This is quite true. It is also quite false. Yes, we were servants. But we were learned servants! And we used our learning to celebrate men's average lives! (*A grand-er music sounds. The* Emperor *remains seated, but the other four men in the Light Box* — Stack, Rosenberg, Van Sweiten *and the* Priest — *come slowly out on to the main stage and process imposingly down it, and around it, and up it again to return to their places. Only the* Priest *goes off, as do* Teresa *on her side, and* Katherina *on hers.*)

Salieri. (*Over this.*) We took unremarkable men: usual bankers, run-of-the-mill priests, ordinary soldiers and statesmen and wives — and sacramentalised their mediocrity. We smoothed their noons with strings *divisi!*, we pierced their nights with *chittarini!* We gave them processions for their strutting — serenades for their rutting — high horns for their hunting, and drums for their wars! Trumpets sounded when they entered the world, and trombones groaned when they left it! The savour of their days remains behind because of *Us*, our music still remembered while their politics are long forgotten. (*The* EMPEROR *hands his rolled paper to* STRACK *and goes off. In the Light Box are left standing, like three icons,* ORSINI-ROSENBERG, *plump and supercilious, aged sixty;* VON STRACK, *stiff and proper, aged fifty-five;* VAN SWIETEN, *cultivated and serious, aged fifty. The lights go down on them a little.*) Tell me, before you call us servants, who served whom? And who I wonder, in your generations, will immortalise *you?* (*The* Two VENTICELLI *come on quickly* D., *from either side. They are now be-wigged also, and are dressed well, in the style of the late eighteenth century. Their manner is more confidential than before.*)

VENTICELLO 1. (*To* SALIERI.) Sir!

VENTICELLO 2. (*To* SALIERI.) Sir!

VENTICELLO 1. Sir. Sir.

VENTICELLO 2. Sir. Sir. Sir. (SALIERI *bids them wait for a second.*)

SALIERI. I was the most successful young musician in the city of musicians. And now suddenly, without warning— (*They approach him eagerly, from either side.*)

VENTICELLO 1. Mozart!

VENTICELLO 2. Mozart!

VENTICELLO 1 & VENTICELLO 2. *Mozart has come!*

SALIERI. These are my Venticelli. My 'Little Winds' as I call them. (*He gives each a coin from his pocket.*) The secret of successful living in a large City is always to know to the minute what is being done behind your back.

VENTICELLO 1. He's left Salzburg.

VENTICELLO 2. Means to give concerts.

VENTICELLO 1. Asking for subscribers.

SALIERI. I'd known of him for years, of course. Tales of his prowess were told all over Europe.

VENTICELLO 1. They say he wrote his first symphony at five.

VENTICELLO 2. I hear his first Concerto at four.

VENTICELLO 1. A full Opera at fourteen.

VENTICELLO 2. Mitradate, King of Pontus.

SALIERI. (*To them.*) How old is he now?

VENTICELLO 2. Twenty-five.

SALIERI. (*Carefully.*) And how long is he remaining?

VENTICELLO 1. He's not departing.

VENTICELLO 2. He's here to stay. (*The* VENTICELLI *glide off.*)

* * * *

The Palace of Schönbrunn.

Lights come up on the three stiff figures of ROSENBERG, STRACK *and* VAN SWIETEN, *standing* U. *in the Light Box. The* CHAMBERLAIN *hands the paper he has received from the* EMPEROR *to the* DIRECTOR OF THE OPERA. SALIERI *remains* D.

STRACK. (*To* ROSENBERG.) You are required to commission a comic opera in German from Herr Mozart.

SALIERI. (*To Audience.*) Johann Von Strack. Royal Chamberlain. A Court official to his collar bone.

ROSENBERG. (*Loftily.*) Why in German? Italian is the only possible language for Opera!

SALIERI. Count Orsini-Rosenberg. Director of the Opera. Benevolent to all things Italian—especially myself.

STRACK. (*Stiffly.*) The idea of a National Opera is

dear to His Majesty's heart. He desires to hear pieces in good plain German.

VAN SWIETEN. Yes, but why comic? It is not the function of music to be funny.

SALIERI. Baron Van Swieten. Prefect of the Imperial Library. Ardent Freemason. Yet to find anything funny. Known for his enthusiasm for old-fashioned music as 'Lord Fugue'.

VAN SWIETEN. I heard last week a remarkable *serious* opera from Mozart: *Idomeneo, King of Crete.*

ROSENBERG. I heard that too. A young fellow trying to impress beyond his abilities. Too much spice. Too many notes.

STRACK. (*Firmly, to* ROSENBERG.) Nevertheless, kindly convey the commission to him today.

ROSENBERG. (*Taking the paper reluctantly.*) I believe we are going to have trouble with this young man. (ROSENBERG *leaves the Light Box and strolls down the stage to* SALIERI.) He was a child prodigy. That always spells trouble. His father is Leopold Mozart, a bad-tempered Salzburg musician who dragged the boy endlessly round Europe making him play the keyboard blindfold, with one finger, and that sort of thing. (*To* SALIERI.) All prodigies are hateful—*non è vero, Compositore?*

SALIERI. *Divengono sempre sterili con gli anni.*

ROSENBERG. *Precisamente. Precisamente.*

STRACK. (*Calling suspiciously.*) What are you saying?

ROSENBERG. (*Airily.*) Nothing, Herr Chamberlain! . . . Niente, Signor Pomposo! . . . (*He strolls on out.* STRACK *strides off irritated.* VAN SWIETEN *now comes* D.)

VAN SWIETEN. We meet tomorrow, I believe, on your Committee to devise pensions for old musicians.

SALIERI. (*Deferentially.*) It's most gracious of you to attend, Baron.

VAN SWIETEN. You're a worthy man, Salieri. You should join our Brotherhood of Masons. We would welcome you warmly.

SALIERI. I would be honoured, Baron!

VAN SWIETEN. If you wished I could arrange initiation into my Lodge.

SALIERI. That would be more than my due.

VAN SWIETEN. Nonsense. We embrace men of talent of all conditions. I may invite young Mozart also: dependent on the impression he makes.

SALIERI. (*Bowing.*) Of course, Baron. (VAN SWIETEN *goes out.*) (*To Audience.*) Honour indeed. In those days almost every man of influence in Vienna was a Mason, — and the Baron's Lodge by far the most fashionable. As for young Mozart, I confess I was alarmed by his coming. Not by the commission of a comic opera, even though I myself was then attempting one called *The Chimney Sweep.* No, what worried me were reports about the man himself. He was praised altogether too much. (*The* VENTICELLI *hurry in from either side.*)

VENTICELLO 1. Such gaiety of spirit!

VENTICELLO 2. Such ease of manner!

VENTICELLO 1. Such natural charm!

SALIERI. Really? Where does he live?

VENTICELLO 1. Peter Platz.

VENTICELLO 2. Number eleven.

VENTICELLO 1. The landlady is Madame Weber.

VENTICELLO 2. A real bitch.

VENTICELLO 1. Takes in male lodgers, and has a tribe of daughters.

VENTICELLO 2. Mozart was engaged to one of them before.

VENTICELLO 1. A soprano called Aloysia.

VENTICELLO 2. She jilted him.

VENTICELLO 1. Now he's after another sister.

VENTICELLO 2. Constanze!

SALIERI. You mean he was actually engaged to one sister and now wants to marry another?

VENTICELLO 1 & VENTICELLO 2. (*Together.*) Exactly!

VENTICELLO 1. Her mother's pushing marriage.

VENTICELLO 2. His *father* isn't!

VENTICELLO 1. Daddy is worried sick!

VENTICELLO 2. Writes him every day from Salzburg!

SALIERI. (*To them.*) I want to meet him.

VENTICELLO 1. He'll be at the Baroness Waldstädten's tomorrow night.

SALIERI. Grazie.

VENTICELLO 2. Some of his music is to be played.

SALIERI. (*To both.*) *Restiamo in contatto.*

VENTICELLO 1 & VENTICELLO 2. *Certamente, Signore!* (*They go off.*)

SALIERI. (*To Audience.*) So to the Baroness Waldstädten's I went. That night changed my life.

* * * *

The Library of the BARONESS WALDSTÄDTEN.

In the Light Box, two elegantly curtained windows surrounded by handsome subdued wallpaper. Two SERVANTS *bring on a large table loaded with cakes and desserts. Two more carry on a grand high-backed wing-chair, which they place ceremoniously* D. *at the* L.

SALIERI. (*To Audience.*) I entered the library to take

first a little refreshment. My generous hostess always put out the most delicious confections in that room whenever she knew I was coming. *Dolce — caramelli —* and most especially a miraculous *crema al mascarpone* — which is simply cream cheese mixed with granulated sugar and suffused with rum — that was totally irresistible! (*He takes a little bowl of it from the cakestand and sits in the wing-chair, facing out front. Thus seated, he is invisible to anyone entering from* u.) I had just sat down in a high-backed chair to consume this paradisal dish — unobservable as it happened to anyone who might come in. (*Offstage, noises are heard.*)

CONSTANZE. (*Off.*) Squeak! Squeak! Squeak! (CONSTANZE *runs on from* u.: *a pretty girl in her early twenties, full of high spirits. At this second she is pretending to be a mouse. She runs across the stage in her gay party dress, and hides under the fortepiano. Suddenly a small, pallid, large-eyed* MAN *in a showy wig and a showy set of clothes runs in after her and freezes — Centre — as a cat would freeze, hunting a mouse. This is* WOLFGANG AMADEUS MOZART. *As we get to know him through his next scenes, we discover several things about him: he is an extremely restless man, his hands and feet in almost continuous motion; his voice is light and high; and he is possessed of an unforgettable giggle — piercing and infantile.*)

MOZART. Miaouw!

CONSTANZE. (*Betraying where she is.*) Squeak!

MOZART. Miaouw! Miaouw! Miaouw! (*The composer drops on all fours and, wrinkling his face, begins spitting and stalking his prey. The mouse — giggling with excitement — breaks her cover and dashes across the floor. The cat pursues. Almost at the chair where* SALIERI *sits concealed, the mouse turns at bay. The cat stalks her—nearer and nearer—in its knee-breeches and elaborate coat.*) I'm going to pounce-bounce! I'm going to scrunch-munch! I'm going to chew-poo my little mouse-wouse! I'm going to tear her to bits with my paws-claws!

CONSTANZE. No!

MOZART. Paws-claws, paws-claws, paws-claws, OHH! . . . (*He falls on her. She screams.*)

SALIERI. (*To Audience.*) Before I could rise, it had become difficult to do so.

MOZART. I'm going to bite you in half with my fangs-wangs! My little Stanzerl-wanzerl-banzerl! (*She giggles delightedly, lying prone beneath him.*) You're trembling! . . . I think you're frightened of puss-wuss! . . . I think you're scared to death! (*Intimately.*) I think you're going to shit yourself! (*She squeals, but is not really shocked.*) In a moment it's going to be on the floor!

CONSTANZE. Ssh! Someone'll hear you! (*He imitates the noise of a fart.*) Stop it, Wolferl! Ssh!

MOZART. Here it comes now! I can hear it *coming!* . . . Oh what a melancholy note! Something's dropping from your boat! (*Another fart noise, slower.* CONSTANZE *shrieks with amusement.*)

CONSTANZE. Stop it now! It's stupid! Really *stupid!* (SALIERI *sits appalled.*)

MOZART. Hey—Hey—what's Trazom!

CONSTANZE. What?

MOZART. T R A Z O M. What's that mean?

CONSTANZE. How should *I* know?

MOZART. It's Mozart spelt backwards—shit-wit! If you ever married me, you'd be Constanze Trazom.

CONSTANZE. No, I wouldn't.

MOZART. Yes, you would. Because I'd want everything backwards once I was married. I'd want to lick my wife's arse instead of her face.

CONSTANZE. You're not going to lick anything at this rate. Your father's never going to give his consent to us. (*The sense of fun deserts him instantly.*)

MOZART. And who cares about his consent?

CONSTANZE. *You* do. You care very much. You wouldn't do it without it.

MOZART. Wouldn't I?

CONSTANZE. No, you wouldn't. Because you're too scared of him. I know what he says about me. (*Solemn voice.*) 'If you marry that dreadful girl, you'll end up lying on straw with beggars for children.'

MOZART. (*Impulsively.*) Marry me!

CONSTANZE. Don't be silly.

MOZART. Marry me!

CONSTANZE. Are you serious?

MOZART. (*Defiantly.*) Yes! . . . Answer me this minute: yes or no! Say yes, then I can go home, climb into bed—shit over the mattress and shout 'I *did* it!' (*He rolls on top of her delightedly, uttering his high whinnying giggle. The* MAJOR-DOMO *of the house stalks in,* U.)

MAJOR-DOMO. (*Imperviously.*) Her Ladyship is ready to commence.

MOZART. Ah! . . . Yes! . . . Good! (*He picks himself up, embarrassed, and helps* CONSTANZE *to rise. With an attempt at dignity.*) Come, my dear. The music waits!

CONSTANZE. (*Suppressing giggles.*) Oh, by all means— Herr Trazom! (*He takes her arm. They prance off together, followed by the disapproving* MAJOR-DOMO.)

SALIERI. (*Shaken: to Audience.*) And then, right away, the concert began. I heard it through the door— some Serenade: at first only vaguely—too horrified to attend. But presently the sound insisted—a solemn Adagio in E flat. (*The Adagio for the Serenade for Thirteen Wind Instruments (K. 361) begins to sound.*

Quietly and quite slowly, seated in the wing-chair, SALIERI *speaks over the music.*) It started simply enough: just a pulse in the lowest registers — bassoons and basset horns — like a rusty squeezebox. It would have been comic except for the slowness, which gave it instead a sort of serenity. And then suddenly, high above it, sounded a single note on the oboe. (*We hear it.*) It hung there unwavering — piercing me through — till breath could hold it no longer, and a clarinet withdrew it out of me, and sweetened it into a phrase of such delight it had me trembling. The light flickered in the room. My eyes clouded! (*With ever-increasing emotion and vigour.*) The squeezebox groaned louder, and over it the higher instruments wailed and warbled, throwing lines of sound around me — long lines of pain around and through me — Ah, the pain! Pain as I had never known it. I called up to my sharp old God *'What is this? . . . What?!'* But the squeezebox went on and on, and the pain cut deeper into my shaking head until suddenly I was running — (*He bolts out of the chair and runs across the stage in a fever, to* C. *[Behind him in the Light Box the Library fades into a`street scene at night: small houses under a torn sky.] The music continues, fainter, underneath.*) — dashing through the side-door, stumbling downstairs into the street, into the cold night, gasping for life. (*Calling up in agony.*) *'What?! What is this? Tell me, Signore!* What is this *pain?* What is this *need* in the sound? Forever unfulfillable yet fulfilling him who hears it, utterly. Is it *Your* need? Can it be Yours? . . .' (*Pause.*) Dimly the music sounded from the salon above. Dimly the stars shone on the empty street. I was suddenly frightened. It seemed to me I had heard a voice of God — and that it issued from a creature whose own voice I had also heard — and it was the voice of an obscene child! (*Light change. The street scene fades.*)

* * * *

SALIERI'S *Apartments.*
It remains dark.

I ran home and buried my fear in work. More pupils—till there were thirty and forty. More Committees—toiling long hours to help musicians! More Motets and Anthems to God's glory. And at night I prayed for just one thing. (*He kneels desperately.*) 'Let your voice enter *me!* Let *me* be your conduct! . . . *Let* me! (*Pause. He rises.*) As for Mozart, I avoided meeting him—and sent out my Little Winds for whatever scores of his could be found. (*The* VENTICELLI *come in with manuscripts.* SALIERI *sits at the fortepiano, and they show him the music alternatively, as* SERVANTS *unobtrusively remove the Waldstädten table and wing-chair.*)

VENTICELLO 1. Six fortepiano Sonatas composed in Munich.

SALIERI. Clever.

VENTICELLO 2. Two in Mannheim.

SALIERI. They were all clever.

VENTICELLO 1. A Parisian Symphony.

SALIERI. (*To Audience.*) And yet they seemed to me completely empty!

VENTICELLO 1. A Divertimento in D.

SALIERI. Same.

VENTICELLO 2. A Cassazione in G.

SALIERI. Conventional.

VENTICELLO 1. A Grand Litany in E Flat.

SALIERI. Even boring. (*To Audience.*) The productions of a precocious youngster—Leopold Mozart's swanky son—nothing more. That Serenade was obviously an exception in his work: the sort of accident which might visit any composer on a lucky day! (*The* VENTICELLI *go off with the music.*) Had I in fact been simply taken by surprise that the filthy creature could write music at all? . . . Suddenly I felt immensely cheered! I would seek him out and welcome him myself to Vienna!

* * * *

The Palace of Schönbrunn.

Quick light change. The EMPEROR *is revealed standing in bright light before the gilded mirrors and the fireplace, attended by* CHAMBERLAIN STRACK. *His Majesty is a dapper, cheerful figure, aged forty, largely pleased with himself and the world.* D.S., *from opposite sides,* VAN SWIETEN *and* ROSENBERG *hurry on.*

JOSEPH. Fêtes and fireworks, gentlemen! Mozart is here! He's waiting below! (*All bow.*)

ALL. Majesty!

JOSEPH. *Je suis follement impatient!*

SALIERI. (*To Audience.*) The Emperor Joseph the Second of Austria. Son of Maria Theresa. Brother of Marie Antionette. Adorer of music—provided that it made no demands upon the royal ear. (*To the* EMPEROR, *deferentially.*) Majesty, I have written a little march in Mozart's honour. May I play it as he comes in?

JOSEPH. By all means, Court Composer. What a delightful idea! Have you met him yet?

SALIERI. Not yet, Majesty.

JOSEPH. Fetes and fireworks, what fun! Strack, bring

him up at once. (STRACK *goes off. The* EMPEROR *comes on to the stage proper.*) *Mon Dieu,* I wish we could have a competition! Mozart against some other virtuoso. Two keyboards in contest. Wouldn't that be fun, Baron?

VAN SWIETEN. (*Stiffly.*) Not to me, Majesty. In my view, musicians are not horses to be run against one another. (*Slight pause.*)

JOSEPH. Ah. Well—there it is. (STRACK *returns.*)

STRACK. Herr Mozart, Majesty.

JOSEPH. Ah! Splendid! . . . (*Conspiratorially he signs to* SALIERI, *who moves quickly to the fortepiano.*) Court Composer—*allons! (To* STRACK.) Admit him, please. (*Instantly* SALIERI *sits at the instrument and strikes up his March on the keyboard. At the same moment* MOZART *struts in, wearing an extremely ornate surcoat, with dress-sword. The* EMPEROR *stands* D.S., C., *his back to the Audience, and as* MOZART *approaches he signs to him to halt and listen. Bewildered,* MOZART *does so—becoming aware of* SALIERI *playing his March of Welcome. It is an extremely banal piece, vaguely—but only vaguely—reminiscent of another march to become very famous later on. All stand in attitudes of listening, until* SALIERI *comes to a finish. Applause.*)

JOSEPH. (*To* SALIERI.) Charming . . . *Comme d'habitude! (He turns and extends his hand to be kissed.*) Mozart. (MOZART *approaches and kneels extravagantly.*)

MOZART. Majesty! Your Majesty's humble slave! Let me kiss your royal hand a hundred thousand times! (*He kisses it greedily, over and over, until its owner withdraws it in embarrassment.*)

JOSEPH. *Non, non, s'il vous plait!* A little less enthusiasm, I beg you. Come sir, *levez-vous! (He assists* MOZART *to rise.*) You will not recall it, but the last time we met you were also on the floor! My sister remembers it to this day. This young man—all of six years old, mind you—slipped on the floor at Schönbrunn—came a nasty purler on his little head . . . Have I told you this before?

ROSENBERG. (*Hastily.*) No, Majesty!

STRACK. (*Hastily.*) No, Majesty!

SALIERI. (*Hastily.*) No, Majesty!

JOSEPH. Well, my sister Antoinette runs forward and picks him up herself. And do you know what he does? Jumps right into her arms—hoopla, just like that!— kisses her on both cheeks and says 'Will you marry me: yes or no?' (*The* COURTIERS *laugh politely.* MOZART *emits his high-pitched giggle. The* EMPEROR *is clearly startled by it.*) I do not mean to embarrass you, Herr Mozart. You know everyone here, surely?

MOZART. Yes, sire. (*Bowing elaborately to* ROSEN- BERG.) Herr Director! (*To* VAN SWIETEN.) Herr Prefect.

JOSEPH. But not, I think, our esteemed Court Com- poser! . . . A most serious omission! No one who cares for art can afford not to know Herr Salieri. He wrote that exquisite little March of Welcome for you.

SALIERI. It was a trifle, Majesty.

JOSEPH. Nevertheless . . .

MOZART. (*To* SALIERI.) I'm overwhelmed, *Signore!*

JOSEPH. Ideas simply pour out of him—don't they, Strack?

STRACK. Endlessly, sire. (*As if tipping him.*) Well done, Salieri.

JOSEPH. Let it be my pleasure then to introduce you! Court Composer Salieri—Herr Mozart of Salzburg!

SALIERI. (*Sleekly, to* MOZART.) *Finalmente. Che gi- oia. Che diletto straordinario.* (*He gives him a prim bow and presents the copy of his music to the* OTHER COMPOSER, *who accepts it with a flood of Italian.*)

MOZART. *Grazie Signore! Mille millione di ben- venuti! Sono commosso! E un onore eccezionale incon-*

trala! Compositore brillante e famossissimo! (*He makes an elaborate and showy bow in return.*)

SALIERI. (*Dryly.*) Grazie.

JOSEPH. Tell me, Mozart, have you received our Commission for the opera?

MOZART. Indeed I have, Majesty! I am so grateful I can hardly speak! . . . I swear to you that you will have the best—the most perfect entertainment ever offered a monarch. I've already found a Libretto.

ROSENBERG. (*Startled.*) Have you? I didn't hear of this!

MOZART. Forgive me, Herr Director, I entirely omitted to tell you.

ROSENBERG. May I ask why?

MOZART. It didn't seem very important.

ROSENBERG. Not important?

MOZART. Not really, no.

ROSENBERG. (*Irritated.*) It is important to *me*, Herr Mozart.

MOZART. (*Embarrassed.*) Yes, I see that. Of course.

ROSENBERG. And who, pray, is it by?

MOZART. Stephanie.

ROSENBERG. A most unpleasant man.

MOZART. But a brilliant writer.

ROSENBERG. (*Coldly.*) Do you think?

MOZART. The story is really amusing, Majesty. The whole plot is set in a—(*He giggles.*)—in a . . . It's set in a . . .

JOSEPH. (*Eagerly.*) Where? Where is it set?

MOZART. It's—it's—rather saucy, Majesty!

JOSEPH. Yes, yes! Where?

MOZART. Well it's actually set in a *seraglio.*

JOSEPH. A what?

MOZART. A pasha's harem. (*He giggles wildly.*)

ROSENBERG. And you imagine that is a suitable subject for performance at a National Theatre?

MOZART. (*In a panic.*) Yes! . . . No! . . . Yes, I mean yes, yes I do. Why not? It's very funny, it's amusing . . . On my honour — Majesty — there's nothing offensive in it. Nothing offensive in the world. It's full of proper German virtues, I swear it! . . .

SALIERI. (*Blandly.*) *Scusate, Signore,* but what are those? Being a foreigner I'm not sure.

JOSEPH. You are being *cattivo*, Court Composer.

SALIERI. Not at all, Majesty.

JOSEPH. Come then, Mozart. Name us a proper German virtue!

MOZART. Love, Sire. I have yet to see that expressed in any Opera.

VAN SWIETEN. Well answered, Mozart.

SALIERI. (*Smiling.*) *Scusate.* I was under the impression one rarely saw anything *else* expressed in Opera.

MOZART. I mean manly love, Signore. Not male sopranos screeching. Or stupid couples rolling their eyes. All that absurd Italian rubbish. (*Pause. Tension.*) I mean the real thing.

JOSEPH. And do you know the real thing yourself, Herr Mozart?

MOZART. Under your pardon, I think I do, Majesty. (*He gives a short giggle.*)

JOSEPH. Bravo. When do you think it will be done?

MOZART. The first act is already finished.

JOSEPH. But it can't be more than two weeks since you started!

MOZART. Composing is not hard when you have the right audience to please, Sire.

VAN SWIETEN. A charming reply, Majesty.

JOSEPH. Indeed, Baron. Fêtes and fireworks! I see we are going to have fêtes and fireworks! *Au revoir Monsieur Mozart. Soyez bienvenu a la court.*

MOZART. (*With expert rapidity.*) *Majesté!—je suis comblé d'honneur d'être accepté dans la maison du Père de tous les musiciens! Servir un monarque aussi plein de discernement que votre Majesté, c'est un honneur qui dépasse le sommet de mes dus!* (*A pause. The* EMPEROR *is taken aback by this flood of French.*)

JOSEPH. Ah. Well—there it is. I'll leave you gentlemen to get better acquainted.

SALIERI. Good day, Majesty.

MOZART. *Votre Majesté.* (*They both bow.* JOSEPH *goes out.*)

ROSENBERG. Good day to you.

STRACK. Good day. (*They follow the King.*)

VAN SWIETEN. (*Warmly shaking his hand.*) Welcome, Mozart. I shall see much more of you. Depend on it!

MOZART. Thank you. (*He bows. The* BARON *goes.* MOZART *and* SALIERI *are left alone.*)

SALIERI. Bene.

MOZART. Bene.

SALIERI. I too wish you success with your opera.

MOZART. I'll have it. It's going to be superb. I must tell you I have already found the most excellent singer for the leading part.

SALIERI. Oh: who is that?

MOZART. Her name is Cavalieri. Katherina Cavalieri. She's really German, but she thinks it will advance her career if she sports an Italian name.

SALIERI. She's quite right. It was my idea. She is in fact my prize pupil. Actually she's a very innocent child. Silly in the way of young singers—but, you know, she's only twenty. (*Without emphasis* MOZART *freezes his movements and* SALIERI *takes one easy step forward to make a fluent aside.*) (*To Audience.*) I had kept my hands off Katherina. Yes! But, I could not bear to think of anyone else's upon her—least of all his!

MOZART. (*Unfreezing.*) You're a good fellow, Salieri! And that's a jolly little thing you wrote for me.

SALIERI. It was my pleasure.

MOZART. Let's see if I can remember it. May I?

SALIERI. By all means. It's yours.

MOZART. *Grazie, Signore.* (MOZART *tosses the manuscript on to the lid of the fortepiano where he cannot see it, sits at the instrument, and plays* SALIERI'S *March of Welcome perfectly from memory—at first slowly, recalling it—but on the reprise of the tune, very much faster.*) The rest is just the same, isn't it? (*He finishes it with insolent speed.*)

SALIERI. You have a remarkable memory.

MOZART. (*Delighted with himself.*) *Grazie ancora,* Signore! (*He plays the opening seven bars again, but this time stops on the interval of the Fourth, and sounds it again with displeasure.*) It doesn't really *work,* that Fourth—does it? . . . Let's try the Third above . . . (*He does so—and smiles happily.*) Ah yes! . . . Good! . . . (*He repeats the new interval, leading up to it smartly with the well-known military-trumpet arpeggio which characterises the celebrated March from* The Marriage of Figaro *'Non piu andrai'. Then, using the interval— tentatively—delicately—one note at a time, in the treble—he steals into the famous tune itself. On and on he plays, improvising happily what is virtually the march we know now, laughing gleefully each time he comes to the amended interval of a Third.* SALIERI *watches him with an answering smile painted on his face.* MOZART'S *playing grows more and more exhibitionistic— revealing to the Audience the formidable virtuoso he is. The whole time he himself remains totally oblivious to the offence he is giving. Finally he finishes the March with a*

*series of triumphant flourishes and chords! An ominous
pause.*)

SALIERI. *Scusate.* I must go.

MOZART. Really? (*Springing up and indicating the
keyboard.*) Why don't *you* try a Variation?

SALIERI. Thank you, but I must attend on the Emperor.

MOZART. Ah.

SALIERI. It has been delightful to meet you.

MOZART. For me too! . . . And thanks for the March!
(MOZART *picks up the manuscript from the top of the
fortepiano and marches happily* O.S. *A slight pause.*
SALIERI *moves towards the Audience. The lights go
down around him.*)

SALIERI. (*To Audience.*) Was it then—so early—that
I began to have thoughts of murder? . . . Of course not:
at least not in Life. In Art it was a different matter. I
decided I would compose a huge tragic opera: something to astonish the world! —and I knew my theme. I
would set the Legend of Danaius, who, for a monstrous
crime was chained to a rock for eternity—his head repeatedly struck by lightning! Wickedly I saw Mozart in
that position. In reality the man was in no danger from
me at all . . . Not yet.

*   *   *   *

The First Performance of
THE ABDUCTION FROM THE SERAGLIO.
*The light changes, and the stage instantly turns into an
    eighteenth-century theatre. The backdrop projection shows a line of softly gleaming chandeliers.*
The SERVANTS *quickly bring in chairs and benches.
    Upon them, facing the Audience and regarding it as*

if watching an opera, sit the EMPEROR JOSEPH, STRACK, ROSENBERG *and* VAN SWIETEN.

Next to them: KAPELLMEISTER BONNO *and* THERESA SALIERI. *A little behind them:* CONSTANZE. *Behind her:* CITIZENS OF VIENNA.

SALIERI. The first performance of The Abduction from The Seraglio. The German expression of manly love. (MOZART *comes on briskly, wearing a gaudy new coat embellished with scarlet ribbons, and a new powdered wig. He struts quickly to the fortepiano, sits at it and mimes conducting.* SALIERI *sits nearby, next to his wife, and watches* MOZART *intently.*) He himself contrived to wear for the occasion an even more vulgar coat than usual. As for the music, it matched the coat completely. For my dear pupil Katherina Cavalieri he had written quite simply the showiest Aria I'd ever heard. (*Faintly we hear the whizzing scale passages for* SOPRANO *which end the Aria 'Marten Aller Arten'.*) Ten minutes of scales and ornaments, amounting in sum to a vast emptiness. So ridiculous was the piece in fact — so much what might be demanded by a foolish young soprano — that I knew precisely what Mozart must have demanded in return for it. (*The final orchestral chords of the Aria. Silence. No one moves.*) Although engaged to be married, *he'd had her!* I knew that beyond any doubt. (*Bluntly.*) The creature had had my darling girl. (*Loudly we hear the brilliant Turkish Finale of 'Seraglio'. Great applause from those watching.* MOZART *jumps to his feet and acknowledges it. The* EMPEROR *rises — as do all — and gestures graciously to the 'stage' in invitation.* KATHERINA CAVALIERI *runs on in her costume, all plumes and flounces, to renewed cheering and clapping. She curtseys to the* EMPEROR — *is kissed by* SALIERI — *presented to his wife — curtseys again to* MOZART *and, flushed with triumph, moves to one side. In the ensuing brief silence* CONSTANZE *rushes down from the back, wildly excited. She flings herself on* MOZART, *not even noticing the* EMPEROR.)

CONSTANZE. Oh, well done, lovey! . . . Well done, pussy-wussy! . . . (MOZART *indicates the proximity of His Majesty.*) Oh! . . . 'Scuse *me!* (*She curtseys in embarrassment.*)

MOZART. Majesty, may I present my fiancée, Fraulein Weber?

JOSEPH. *Enchanté, Fraulein!*

CONSTANZE. Your Majesty!

MOZART. Constanze is a singer herself.

JOSEPH. Indeed?

CONSTANZE. (*Embarrassed.*) I'm not at all, Majesty. Don't be silly, Wolfgang!

JOSEPH. So, Mozart — a good effort. Decidedly that. A good effort.

MOZART. Did you really like it, Sire?

JOSEPH. I thought it was most interesting. Yes, indeed. A trifle — how shall one say? (*To* ROSENBERG.) How shall one say, Director?

ROSENBERG. (*Subserviently.*) Too many notes, Your Majesty?

JOSEPH. Very well put. Too many notes.

MOZART. I don't understand.

JOSEPH. My dear fellow, don't take it too hard. There are in fact only so many notes the ear can hear in the course of an evening. I think I'm right in saying that, aren't I, Court Composer?

SALIERI. (*Uncomfortably.*) Well yes, I would say yes, on the whole, yes, Majesty.

JOSEPH. There you are. It's clever. It's German. It's quality work. And there are simply too many notes. Do you see?

MOZART. There are just as many notes, Majesty,

neither more nor less, as are required. (*Pause.*)

JOSEPH. Ah . . . Well, there it is. (*He goes off abruptly, followed by* ROSENBERG *and* STRACK. *All others go off, save* CONSTANZE *and* MOZART *— who detains* SALIERI.)

MOZART. (*Nervous.*) Herr Salieri,-is he angry?

SALIERI. Not at all. He respects you for your views.

MOZART. (*Nervously.*) I hope so . . . What did you think yourself, sir? Did you care for the piece at all?

SALIERI. Yes, of course, Mozart — at its best it is truly charming.

MOZART. And at other times?

SALIERI. (*Smoothly.*) Well, just occasionally at other times — in Katherina's Aria for example — it was a little excessive.

MOZART. Katherina is an excessive girl. In fact she's insatiable . . . I mean in regard to vocal ornaments.

SALIERI. All the same, as my revered teacher the Chevalier Gluck used to say to me — one must avoid music that smells of music.

MOZART. What does that mean?

SALIERI. Music which makes one aware too much of the virtuosity of the composer.

MOZART. Gluck is absurd.

SALIERI. What do you say?

MOZART. He's talked all his life about modernising opera, but creates people so lofty they sound as though they shit marble. (CONSTANZE *gives a little scream of shock.*)

CONSTANZE. Oh, 'scuse me! . . .

MOZART. (*Breaking out.*) No, but it's too much! Gluck says! Gluck says! Chevalier Gluck! What's Chevalier? I'm a Chevalier. The Pope made me a Chevalier when I was still wetting my bed.

CONSTANZE. Wolferl!

MOZART. Anyway it's ridiculous. Only stupid farts use titles.

SALIERI. (*Blandly.*) Such as Court Composer?

MOZART. What? . . . (*Realising.*) Ah. Oh. Ha. Ha. Well! . . . My father's right again. He always tells me I should padlock my mouth . . . Actually, I shouldn't speak at all!

SALIERI. (*Soothingly.*) Nonsense. I'm just being what the Emperor would call *Cattivo*. Won't you introduce me to your charming fiancee?

MOZART. Oh, of course! Constanze, this is Herr Court Composer Salieri, Fraulein Weber.

SALIERI. (*Bowing.*) Delighted, *cara Fraulein.*

CONSTANZE. (*Bobbing.*) How do you do, Excellency?

SALIERI. You are the sister of Aloysia Weber, the Soprano, are you not?

CONSTANZE. I am, Excellency.

SALIERI. A beauty herself, but you exceed her by far, if I may observe so.

CONSTANZE. Oh, thank you!

SALIERI. May I ask when you marry?

MOZART. (*Nervously.*) We have to secure my father's consent. He's an excellent man — a wonderful man — but in some ways a little stubborn.

SALIERI. Excuse me, but how old are you?

MOZART. Twenty-six.

SALIERI. Then your father's consent is scarcely indispensable.

CONSTANZE. (*To* MOZART.) You see?

MOZART. (*Uncomfortably.*) Well no, it's not indispensable — of course not! . . .

SALIERI. My advice to you is to marry and be happy. You have found — it's quite obvious — *un tesoro raro!*

CONSTANZE. Ta very much.

SALIERI. (*He kisses* CONSTANZE's *hand. She is delighted.*) Good night to you both.

CONSTANZE. Goodnight, Excellency!

MOZART. Goodnight, sir. And thank you . . . Come, Stanzerl. (*They depart delightedly. He watches them go.*)

SALIERI. (*To Audience.*) As I watched her walk away on the arm of the Creature, I felt the lightning thought strike—'*Have her! Her for Katherina!*' . . . Abomination! . . . Never in my life had I entertained a notion so sinful! (*Light change: the eighteenth-century fades. The* VENTICELLI *come on merrily, as if from some celebration.* ONE *holds a bottle; the* OTHER *a glass.*)

VENTICELLO 1. They're married.

SALIERI. (*To them.*) What?

VENTICELLO 2. Mozart and Weber—married!

SALIERI. Really?

VENTICELLO 1. His father will be furious!

VENTICELLO 2. They didn't even wait for his consent!

SALIERI. Have they set up house?

VENTICELLO 1. Wipplingerstrasse.

VENTICELLO 2. Number twelve.

VENTICELLO 1. Not bad.

VENTICELLO 2. Considering they've no money.

SALIERI. Is that really true?

VENTICELLO 1. He's wildly extravagant.

VENTICELLO 2. Lives way beyond his means.

SALIERI. But he has pupils.

VENTICELLO 1. Only three.

SALIERI. (*To them.*) Why so few?

VENTICELLO 1. He's embarrassing.

VENTICELLO 2. Makes scenes.

VENTICELLO 1. Makes enemies.

VENTICELLO 2. Even Strack, whom he cultivates.

SALIERI. Chamberlain Strack?

VENTICELLO 1. Only last night.

VENTICELLO 2. At Kapellmeister Bonno's.

* * * *

BONNO's *House.*

Instant light change. MOZART *comes in with* STRACK. *He is high on wine, and holding a glass. The* VENTI-CELLI *join the Scene, but still talk out of it to* SALIERI. *One of them fills* MOZART's *glass.*

MOZART. Seven months in this City and not one job! I'm not to be tried again, is that it?

STRACK. Of course it isn't.

MOZART. I know what goes on,—and so do you. Vienna is completely in the hands of foreigners. Worthless wops like *Kapellmeister Bonno!*

STRACK. Please! You're in the man's house!

MOZART. Court Composer *Salieri!*

STRACK. Hush!

MOZART. Did you see his last opera?—'The Chimney Sweep'? . . . Did you?

STRACK. Of course I did.

MOZART. Dogshit! . . . *Dried* dogshit.

STRACK. (*Outraged.*) I beg your pardon!

MOZART. (*Playing the harpsichord and singing.*) Pom-pom, pom-pom, pom-pom! Tonic and dominant, tonic and dominant from here to resurrection! Not one interesting modulation all night. Salieri is a musical idiot!

STRACK. Please!

[VENTICELLO 1. (*To* SALIERI.) He'd had too much to drink.]

[VENTICELLO 2. He often has.]

MOZART. Why are Italians so terrified by the slightest complexity in music? Show them one chromatic passage and they *faint!* . . . 'Oh how sick!' 'How morbid!' (*Fal-*

setto.) *Morboso!* . . . *Nervoso!* . . . Ohimè! . . . No wonder the music at this court is so dreary.

STRACK. Lower your voice.

MOZART. Lower your breeches! . . . That's just a joke — just a joke! (*Unobserved by him* COUNT ROSENBERG *has entered* U.S. *and is suddenly standing between the* VENTICELLI, *listening. He wears a waistcoat of bright green silk, and an expression of supercilious interest.* MOZART *sees him. A pause. Pleasantly, to* ROSENBERG.) You look like a toad . . . I mean you're goggling like a toad. (*He giggles.*)

ROSENBERG. (*Blandly.*) You would do best to retire tonight, for your own sake.

MOZART. Salieri has fifty pupils. I have three. How am I to live? I'm a married man now! . . . Of course I realise you don't concern yourselves with *money* in these exalted circles. All the same, did you know behind his back His Majesty is known as Kaiser Keep it? (*He giggles wildly.*)

STRACK. *Mozart!* (*He stops.*)

MOZART. I shouldn't have said that, should I? Forgive me. It was just a joke. Another joke! . . . I can't help myself! . . . We're all friends here, aren't we? (STRACK *and* ROSENBERG *glare at him. Then* STRACK *leaves abruptly, much offended.*) What's wrong with *him*?

ROSENBERG. Goodnight. (*He turns to go.*)

MOZART. No, no, no — please! (*He grabs the* DIRECTOR'S *arm.*) Your hand please, first! (*Unwillingly* ROSENBERG *gives him his hand.* MOZART *kisses it. Humbly.*) Give me a Post, sir.

ROSENBERG. That is not in my power, Mozart.

MOZART. The Princess Elizabeth is looking for an Instructor. One word from you could secure it for me.

ROSENBERG. I regret that is solely in the recommendation of Court Composer Salieri. (*He disengages himself.*)

MOZART. Do you know I am better than any musician in Vienna? . . . Do you? (*Silence. The* VENTICELLI *are left looking at him, smiling.*) The devil take the lot of them! . . . Nothing but cabals and cliques everywhere you look! What's here for an honest German fellow? (*He becomes aware of the* VENTICELLI, *and makes an attempt at dignity. He sings (Tune of La ci darem).*)
"The girl who doesn't like me—
The girl who doesn't like me—
The girl who doesn't like me—
Can lick my arse instead!"
(*He struts off, holding his head high.*)

SALIERI. (*Watching him go.*) Barely one month later, that thought of revenge became more than thought.

****

The Waldstädten Library.
Two simultaneous shouts bring up the lights. Against the handsome wallpaper stand three masked figures: CONSTANZE, *flanked on either side by the* VENTICELLI. *All three are guests at a party, and are playing a game of forfeits.* TWO SERVANTS *stand frozen, holding the large wingchair between them.* TWO MORE *hold the big table of sweetmeats.*)

VENTICELLO 1. Forfeit! . . . Forfeit! . . .

VENTICELLO 2. Forfeit, Stanzerl! You've got to forfeit!

CONSTANZE. I won't.

VENTICELLO 1. You have to.

VENTICELLO 2. It's the game. (*The* SERVANTS *unfreeze and set down the furniture.* SALIERI *moves to the wing-chair and sits.*)

SALIERI. (*To Audience.*) Once again—believe it or not—I was in the same concealing chair in the Baroness' Library—(*Taking a cup from the little table.*) and consuming the same delicious dessert.

VENTICELLO 1. You lost—now there's the penalty!

SALIERI. (*To Audience.*) A party celebrating the New Year's Eve. I was on my own—my dear spouse Teresa visiting her parents in Italy.

CONSTANZE. Well, *what*? . . . What is it? (VENTICELLO ONE *snatches up an old-fashioned round ruler from off the fortepiano.*)

VENTICELLO 1. I want to measure your calves.

CONSTANZE. Oooo!

VENTICELLO 1. Well?

CONSTANZE. Definitely not. You cheeky bugger!

VENTICELLO 1. Now come on!

VENTICELLO 2. You've got to let him, Stanzerl. All's fair in love and forfeits.

CONSTANZE. No it isn't—so you can both buzz off!

VENTICELLO 1. If you don't let me, you won't be allowed to play again.

CONSTANZE. Well choose something else.

VENTICELLO 1. I've chosen that. Now get up on the table. Quick, quick! *Allez-oop!* (*Gleefully he shifts the plates of sweetmeats from the table.*)

CONSTANZE. Quick, then! . . . Before anyone sees! (*The* TWO *masked men lift the shrieking masked girl up on to the table.*)

VENTICELLO 1. Hold her, Friedrich.

CONSTANZE. I don't have to be held, thank you!

VENTICELLO 2. Yes, you do: that's part of the penalty.

(*He holds her ankles firmly, whilst* VENTICELLO ONE *thrusts the ruler under her skirts and measures her legs. Excitedly* SALIERI *reverses his position so that he can kneel in the wing-chair, and watch.* CONSTANZE *giggles delightedly, then becomes outraged—or pretends to be.*)

CONSTANZE. Stop it! . . . Stop that! That's quite enough of that! (*She bends down and tries to slap him.*)

VENTICELLO 1. Seventeen inches—knee to ankle!

VENTICELLO 2. Let me, Karl! You hold her.

CONSTANZE. That's not fair!

VENTICELLO 2. Yes, it is. You lost to me too.

CONSTANZE. It's been done now! Let me *down*!

VENTICELLO 2. Hold her, Karl.

CONSTANZE. No! . . . (VENTICELLO ONE *holds her ankles.* VENTICELLO TWO *thrusts his head entirely under her skirts. She squeals.*) No—stop it! . . . *No!* . . . (*In the middle of this undignified scene* MOZART *comes rushing on—also masked.*)

MOZART. (*Outraged.*) Constanze! (*They freeze.* SALIERI *ducks back down and sits hidden in the chair.*) Gentlemen, if you please.

CONSTANZE. It's only a game, Wolferl! . . .

VENTICELLO 1. We meant no harm, 'pon my word.

MOZART. (*Stiffly.*) Come down off that table please. (*They hand her down.*) Thank you. We'll see you later.

VENTICELLO 2. Now look, Mozart, don't be pompous—

MOZART. Please excuse us *now*! (*They go. The little man is very angry. He tears off his mask.*) (*To* CONSTANZE.) Do you realise what you've done?

CONSTANZE. No, what? . . . (*Flustered, she busies herself restoring the plates of sweetmeats to the table.*)

MOZART. Just lost your reputation, that's all! You're

now a loose girl.

CONSTANZE. Don't be so stupid. (*She too removes her mask.*)

MOZART. You are a married woman, for God's sake!

CONSTANZE. And what of it?

MOZART. A young wife does not allow her legs to be handled in public. Couldn't you at least have measured your own ugly legs?

CONSTANZE. *What?* Of course they're not as good as Aloysia's. My sister had perfect legs, we all know that.

MOZART. (*Raising his voice.*) Do you know what you've done?! . . . You've shamed me—that's all! *Shamed* me!

CONSTANZE. Oh, don't be so ridiculous!

MOZART. Shamed me—in front of *them*!

CONSTANZE. (*Suddenly furious.*) You—shamed *you?* . . . That's a laugh! If there's any shame around, lovey, it's *mine!*

MOZART. What do you mean?

CONSTANZE. You've only had every pupil who ever came to you.

MOZART. That's not true.

CONSTANZE. Every single female pupil!

MOZART. Name them! *Name them!*

CONSTANZE. The Aurnhammer girl! The Rumbeck girl! Katherina Cavalieri—that sly little whore! *She* wasn't even your pupil—she was Salieri's. Which actually, my dear, may be why he has hundreds and you have none! He doesn't drag them into bed!

MOZART. Of course he doesn't! He can't get it up, that's why! . . . Have you heard his music? That's the sound of someone who *can't get it up!* At least *I* can do that!

CONSTANZE. I'm sick of you!

MOZART. (*Shouting.*) No one ever said I couldn't do *that!*

CONSTANZE. (*Bursting into tears.*) I don't give a fart! I hate you! I hate you for ever and ever — I hate you! (*A tiny pause. She weeps.*)

MOZART. (*Helplessly.*) Oh Stanzerl, don't cry. Please don't cry . . . I can't bear it when you cry. I just didn't want you to look cheap in people's eyes, that's all. Here! (*He snatches up the ruler.*) Beat me. Beat me . . . I'm your slave. Stanzi marini! . . . Stanzi marini bini gini! . . . I'll just stand here like a little lamb and bear your strokes. Here. Do it . . . *Batti.*

CONSTANZE. No.

MOZART. *Batti, batti. Mio tesoro!*

CONSTANZE. No!

MOZART. Stanzerly wanzerly piggly poo!

CONSTANZE. Stop it.

MOZART. Stanzy wanzy had a fit. Shit her stays and made them split!

CONSTANZE. (*She giggles despite herself.*) Stop it.

MOZART. When they took away her skirt, Stanzy wanzy ate the dirt!

CONSTANZE. Stop it now! (*She snatches the ruler and gives him a whack with it. He yowls playfully.*)

MOZART. Oooo! Oooo! Oooo! Do it again! Do it again! I cast myself at your stinking feet, Madonna! (*He does so. She whacks him some more as he crouches, but always lightly, scarcely looking at him, divided between tears and laughter. MOZART drums his feet with pleasure.*)

MOZART. Ow! Ow! Ow! (*And then suddenly SALIERI, unable to bear another second, cries out involuntarily.*)

SALIERI. *Ah!!!* (*The young couple freezes. SALIERI — discovered — hastily converts his noise of disgust into a yawn, and stretches as if waking up from a nap. He peers out of the wing-chair.*) Good evening.

CONSTANZE. (*Embarrassed.*) Excellency . . .

MOZART. How long have you been there?

SALIERI. I was asleep until a second ago. Are you two quarrelling?

MOZART. No, of course not.

CONSTANZE. Yes, we are. He's been very irritating.

SALIERI. (*Rising.*) Caro Herr, tonight is the time for New Year resolutions. Irritating lovely ladies cannot surely be one of yours. May I suggest you bring us each a sorbetto from the dining-room?

MOZART. But why don't we all go to the table?

CONSTANZE. Herr Salieri is quite right. Bring them here — it'll be your punishment.

MOZART. Stanzi!

SALIERI. Come now, I can keep your wife company. There cannot be a better peace offering than a sorbetto of almonds.

CONSTANZE. I prefer tangerine.

SALIERI. Very well, tangerine. (*Greedily.*) But if you could possibly manage almonds for me, I'd be deeply obliged . . . So the New Year can begin coolly for all three of us. (*A pause.* MOZART *hesitates — and then bows.*)

MOZART. I'm honoured, Signore, of course. And then I'll play you at billiards. What do you say?

SALIERI. I'm afraid I don't play.

MOZART. (*With surprise.*) You don't?

CONSTANZE. Wolferl would rather play at billiards than anything. He's very good at it.

MOZART. I'm the best! I may nod occasionally at composing, but at billiards — never!

SALIERI. A virtuoso of the cue.

MOZART. Exactly! It's a virtuoso's game! . . . (*He snatches up the ruler and treats it as if it were a cue.*) I think I shall write a Grand Fantasia for Billiard Balls! Trillos. Accacciatures! Whole arpeggios in ivory! Then

I'll play it myself in public! . . . It'll have to be *me* because none of those Italian charlatans like Clementi will be able to get his fingers round the cue! (*Hostile.*) *Scusate, Signore!* (*He gives a swanky flourish of the hand and struts off.*)

CONSTANZE. (*Nervously.*) He's a love, really.

SALIERI. And lucky, too, in you. You are, if I may say so, an astonishing creature.

CONSTANZE. Me? . . . Ta very much.

SALIERI. On the other hand, your husband does not appear to be so thriving.

CONSTANZE. (*Seizing her opportunity.*) We're desperate, sir.

SALIERI. What?

CONSTANZE. We've no money and no prospects of any. That's the truth.

SALIERI. I don't understand. He gives many public concerts.

CONSTANZE. They don't pay enough. What he needs is pupils. Illustrious pupils. His father calls us spendthrifts, but that's unfair. I manage as well as anyone could. There's simply not enough. Don't tell him I talked to you, please.

SALIERI. (*Intimately.*) This is solely between us. How can I help?

CONSTANZE. My husband needs security, sir. If only he could find regular employment, everything would be all right. Is there nothing at Court?

SALIERI. Not at the moment.

CONSTANZE. (*Harder.*) The Princess Elizabeth needs a tutor.

SALIERI. Really? I hadn't heard.

CONSTANZE. One word from you and the post would be his. Other pupils would follow at once.

SALIERI. (*Looking off.*) He's coming back.

CONSTANZE. Please . . . please, Excellency. You can't imagine what a difference it would make.

SALIERI. We can't speak of it now.

CONSTANZE. When then? Oh, please!

SALIERI. Can you come and see me tomorrow? Alone?

CONSTANZE. I can't do that.

SALIERI. I'm a married man.

CONSTANZE. All the same.

SALIERI. When does he work?

CONSTANZE. Afternoons.

SALIERI. Then come at three.

CONSTANZE. I can't possibly!

SALIERI. Yes or no? In his interests? (*A pause. She hesitates—opens her mouth—then smiles and abruptly runs off. The curtains fall in the light box. To Audience.*) So I'd done it. Spoken aloud. Invited her! What of that vow made in Church? Virtue . . . Chastity, all of that? What did she think of me—this careful Italian? Sincere friend or hopeful seducer? Would she come? I had no idea! (SERVANTS *remove the Waldstädten furniture. Others replace it with two small gilded chairs,* C., *quite close together. Others again surreptitiously in the old dressing-gown which* SALIERI *discarded before Scene Three, placing them on the fortepiano.*)

***

SALIERI's *Salon.*
On the curtains are thrown again projections of long windows.

SALIERI. If she did, how would I behave? I had no idea of that either . . . Next afternoon I waited in a fever! Was I actually going to seduce a young wife of

two month's standing? . . . Part of me—much of me—
wanted it, badly. Badly. Yes, badly was the word! . . .
(*The clock strikes three. On the first stroke the bell
sounds. He rises excitedly.*) There she was! On the
stroke! She'd come . . . She'd *come!* (*Enter from the* R.
the COOK, *still as fat, but forty years younger. He proudly
carries a plate piled with brandied chestnuts.* SALIERI
*takes them from him nervously, nodding with approval,
and sets them on the table.*) (*To the* COOK.) Grazie.
Grazie tanti . . . Via, via, via! (*The* COOK *bows as* SA-
LIERI *dismisses him, and goes out the same way. The*
VALET *comes in from the* L.,—*he is also forty years
younger—and behind him* CONSTANZE, *wearing a pretty
hat and carrying a portfolio.*) Signora!

CONSTANZE. (*Curtseying.*) Excellency.

SALIERI. Benvenuta. (*To* VALET *in dismissal.*) Grazie.
(*The* VALET *goes.*) Well. You have come.

CONSTANZE. I should not have done. My husband
would be frantic if he knew. He's a very jealous man.

SALIERI. Are you a jealous woman?

CONSTANZE. Why do you ask?

SALIERI. It's not a passion I understand . . . You're
looking even prettier than you were last night, if I may
say so.

CONSTANZE. Ta very much! . . . I brought you some
manuscripts by Wolfgang. When you see them you'll
undersand how right he is for a Royal Appointment.
Will you look at them, please, while I wait?

SALIERI. You mean now?

CONSTANZE. Yes, I have to take them back with me.
He'll miss them otherwise. He doesn't make copies.
These are all the originals.

SALIERI. Sit down. Let me offer you something
special.

CONSTANZE. (*Sitting.*) What's that?

SALIERI. (*Producing the box.*) *Capezzoli di Venere.*
Nipples of Venus. Roman chestnuts in brandied sugar.

CONSTANZE. No, thank you.

SALIERI. Do try. They were made especially for you.

CONSTANZE. Me?

SALIERI. Yes.

CONSTANZE. Well then, I'd better hadn't I? Just one . . .
Ta very much. (*She takes one and puts it in her mouth.
The taste amazes her.*) Oh! . . . Oh! . . . Oh! . . .
They're *delish!*

SALIERI. (*Lustfully watching her eat.*) Aren't they?

CONSTANZE. Mmmmm!

SALIERI. Have another.

CONSTANZE. (*Taking two more.*) I couldn't possibly.
(*Carefully he moves round behind her, and seats himself on the chair next to her.*)

SALIERI. I think you're the most generous girl in the
world.

CONSTANZE. Generous?

SALIERI. It's my word for you. I thought last night
that Constanze is altogether too stiff a name for that
girl. I shall rechristen her 'Generosa'. *La Generosa.*
Then I'll write a glorious song for her under that title
and she'll sing it, just for me.

CONSTANZE. (*Smiling.*) My sister's the singer,
sir.

SALIERI. *La Generosa. (He leans a little towards her.*)
Don't tell me it's going to prove inaccurate, my name for
you.

CONSTANZE. (*Coolly.*) What name do you give your
wife, Excellency?

SALIERI. (*Equally coolly.*) I'm not an Excellency, and
I call my wife Signora Salieri. If I named her anything
else it would be *La Statua.* She's a very upright lady.

CONSTANZE. Is she here now? I'd like to meet her.

SALIERI. Alas, no. At the moment she's visiting her mother in Verona. (*She starts very slightly out of her chair.* SALIERI *gently restrains her.*) Constanze: tomorrow evening I dine with the Emperor. One word from me recommending your husband as Tutor to the Princess Elizabeth, and that invaluable post is his. Believe me, when I speak to His Majesty in matters musical, no one contradicts me.

CONSTANZE. I believe you.

SALIERI. *Bene.* (*Still sitting, he takes his mouchoir and delicately wipes her mouth with it.*) Surely service of that sort deserves a little recompense in return?

CONSTANZE. How little? (*Slight pause.*)

SALIERI. The size of a kiss. (*Slight pause.*)

CONSTANZE. Just one? (*Slight pause.*)

SALIERI. If one seems fair to you. (*She looks at him—then kisses him lightly on the mouth. Longer pause.*) Does it? (*She gives him a longer kiss. He makes to touch her with his hand. She breaks off.*)

CONSTANZE. I fancy that's fairness enough. (*Pause.*)

SALIERI. (*Carefully.*) A pity . . . It's somewhat small pay, to secure a post every musician in Vienna is hoping for.

CONSTANZE. What do you mean?

SALIERI. Is it not clear?

CONSTANZE. No. Not at all.

SALIERI. Another pity . . . A thousand pities. (*Pause.*)

CONSTANZE. I don't believe it . . . I just don't believe it!

SALIERI. What?

CONSTANZE. What you've just said.

SALIERI. (*Hastily.*) I said nothing. What did I say?

(CONSTANZE *gets up and* SALIERI *rises in panic.*)

CONSTANZE. Oh, I'm going! . . . I'm getting out of this!

SALIERI. Constanze . . .

CONSTANZE. Let me pass, please.

SALIERI. Constanze, listen to me! I'm a clumsy man. You think me sophisticated — I'm not at all. Take a true look. I've no cunning. I live on ink and sweetmeats. I never see women at all . . . When I met you last night, I envied Mozart from the depths of my soul. Out of that envy came stupid thoughts. For one silly second I dared imagine that — out of the vast store you obviously possess — you might spare me one coin of tenderness your rich husband does not need — and inspire me also. (*Pause. She laughs.*) I amuse.

CONSTANZE. Mozart was right. You're wicked.

SALIERI. He said that?

CONSTANZE. 'All wops are performers,' he said. 'Be very careful with that one.' Meaning you. He was being comic of course.

SALIERI. Yes. (*Abruptly he turns his back on her.*)

CONSTANZE. But not that comic, actually. I mean you're acting a pretty obvious role aren't you, dear? A small town boy, and all the time as clever as cutlets! . . . (*Mock tender.*) Ah! — you are sulking? *Are* you? . . . When Mozart sulks I smack his botty. He rather likes it. Do you want me to scold you a bit and smack your botty too? (*She hits him lightly with the portfolio. He turns in a fury.*)

SALIERI. How dare you?! . . . *You silly, common girl!* (*A dreadful silence.*) (*Icy.*) Forgive me. Let us confine our talk to your husband. He is a brilliant keyboard player, no question. However the Princess Elizabeth also requires a tutor in vocal music. I am not convinced he is the man for that. I would like to look at the pieces you've brought, and decide if he is mature enough. I will study them overnight — and you will study my proposal. Not to be vague: that is the price. (*He extends his hand for the portfolio, and she surrenders it.*) Good afternoon. (*He turns from her and places it on a chair. She lingers — tries to speak — cannot — and goes out quickly.*)

* * * *

The same.
SALIERI *turns in a ferment to the Audience.*

SALIERI. Fiasco! . . . Fiasco! . . . The sordidness of it! The sheer sweating sordidness! . . . Worse than if I'd actually done it! . . . To be that much in sin and feel so *ridiculous* as well! . . . [I didn't deserve any pity from the Old Bargainer above! There was no excuse. If now my music was rejected by Him forever, it was my fault, mine alone.] Would she return tomorrow? Never. And if she did, what then? What would I do? (*Brutally.*) What would I actually *do?* . . . Apologise profoundly — or try again? . . . (*Crying out.*) *Nobilè, nobilè Salieri!* . . . What had he done to me — this Mozart! Before he came did I behave like this? [Did I?] Toy with adultery? Blackmail women? It was all going — slipping — growing rotten — because of *him!* (*He moves* U.S. *in a fever — reaches out to take the portfolio on the chair — but as if fearful of what he might find inside it he withdraws his hand and sits instead. A pause. He contemplates the music lying there as if it were a great confection he is dying to eat, but dare not. Then suddenly he snatches at it — tears the ribbon — opens the case and stares greedily at the manuscripts within. Music sounds instantly, faintly, in the theatre, as his eye falls on the first page. It is the opening of the Twenty-Ninth Symphony, in A Major. Over the music, reading it.*) She had said that these were his original scores. First and only drafts of the music. Yet they looked like fair copies. They showed no corrections of any kind. (*He looks up from the manuscript at the Audience: the music abruptly stops.*) It was puzzling — then suddenly alarming. What was evident was that Mozart was simply transcribing music — (*He resumes looking at the music. Immediately the Sinfonia Concertante for Violin and Viola sounds faintly.*) — completely finished in his head. And finished as most music is never finished. (*He looks up again: the music breaks off.*) Displace one note and there would be diminishment. Displace one phrase and the structure would fall. (*He resumes reading, and the music also resumes: a ravishing phrase from the slow movement of the Concerto for Flute and Harp.*) Here again — only now in abundance — were the same sounds I'd heard in the Library. The same crushed harmonies — glancing collisions — agonising delights. (*And he looks up: again the music stops.*) The truth was clear. That Serenade had been no accident. (*Very low, in the theatre, a faint thundery sound is heard accumulating, like a distant sea.*) I was staring through the cage of those meticulous ink strokes at an Absolute Beauty! (*And out of the thundery roar writhes and rises the clear sound of a* Soprano, *singing the Kyrie from the C Minor Mass. The accretion of noise around her voice falls away — it is suddenly clear and bright — then clearer and brighter. The light grows bright: too bright: burning white, then scalding white!* Salieri *rises in the downpour of it, and*

*in the flood of the music which is growing ever louder—
filling the theatre—as the* SOPRANO *yields to the full*
CHORUS, *fortissimo, singing its massive counterpoint.
This is by far the loudest sound the Audience has yet
heard.* SALIERI *staggers towards us, holding the manuscripts in his hand, like a man caught in a tumbling and
violent sea. Finally the drums crash in below:* SALIERI
*drops the portfolio of manuscripts—and falls senseless
to the ground. At the same second the music explodes
into a long, echoing, distorted boom, signifying some
dreadful annihilation. The sound remains suspended
over the prone* FIGURE *in a menacing continuum—no
longer music at all. Then it dies away, and there is
only silence. The light fades again. A long pause.* SALIERI
*quite still, his head by the pile of manuscripts. Finally
the clock sounds: nine times.* SALIERI *stirs as it does.
Slowly he raises his head and looks up. And now—
quietly at first—he addresses his God.*)

SALIERI. *Capisco!* I know my fate. Now for the first
time I feel my emptiness as Adam felt his nakedness . . .
(*Slowly he rises to his feet.*) Tonight at an inn
somewhere in this city stands a giggling child who can
put on paper, without actually setting down his billiard
cue, casual notes which turn my most considered ones
into lifeless scratches. *Grazie Signore!* You gave me the
desire to serve you—which most men do not have—then
saw to it the service was shameful in the ears of the
server. *Grazie!* You gave me the desire to praise you—
which most do not feel—then made me mute. *Grazie
tanti!* You put into me perception of the Incompara-
ble—which most men never know!—then ensured that I
would know myself forever mediocre. (*His voice gains
power.*) *Why?* . . . *What is my fault?* . . . Until this
day I have pursued virtue with rigour. I have laboured

long hours to relieve my fellow men. I have worked and
worked the talent you allowed me. (*Calling up.*) *You
know how hard I've worked!* — Solely that in the end, in
the practice of the art which alone makes the world
comprehensible to me, I might hear Your Voice! And
now I do hear it — and it says only one name: MOZART!
. . . Spiteful, sniggering, conceited, infantine
Mozart! — who has never worked one minute to help
another man! — shit-talking Mozart with his botty-
smacking wife! — *him* you have chosen to be your sole
conduct! And *my* only reward — my sublime privilege — is
to be the sole man alive in this time who shall clearly
recognise your Incarnation! (*Savagely.*) *Grazie e grazie
anchora!* (*Pause.*) So be it! From this time we are
enemies, You and I! I'll not accept it from You — *Do
you hear? . . .* They say God is not mocked. I tell you,
Man is not mocked! . . . *I* am not mocked! . . . They
say the spirit bloweth where it listeth: I tell you No! It
must list to virtue or not blow at all! (*Yelling.*) *Dio In-
giusto!* — You are the Enemy! I name Thee now — *Nemico
Eterno!* And this I swear. To my last breath I shall *block*
you on earth, as far as I am able! (*He glares up at God.*)
(*To Audience.*) What use, after all, is Man, if not to
teach God His lessons? (*Pause. Suddenly he speaks again
to us in the voice of an old man.*) And now — (*He slips
off his powdered wig, crosses to the fortepiano and takes
from its lid where lie the old dressing-gown, cap and
shawl which he discarded when he conducted us back to
the eighteenth century. These he slips on over his court
coat. It is again 1823.*) before I tell you what happened
next — God's answer to me — and indeed Constanze's —
and all the horrors that followed — let me stop. The
bladder, being a human appendage, is not something
you ghosts need concern yourselves with yet. I being

alive, though barely, am at its constant call. [It is now one hour before dawn— when I must dismiss us both.] When I return I'll tell you about the war I fought with God through his preferred Creature— Mozart, named *Amadeus.* In the waging of which, of course, the Creature had to be destroyed. (*He bows to the Audience with malignant slyness—snatches a pastry from the stand—and leaves the stage, chewing at it voraciously. The manuscripts lie where he spilled them in his fall. The lights in the theatre come up as he goes.*)

END OF ACT I

AMADEUS

ACT TWO

SALIERI's *Salon.*
The lights go down in the theatre as SALIERI *returns.*

SALIERI. I have been listening to the cats in the courtyard. They are all singing Rossini. It is obvious that cats have declined as badly as composers. Domenico Scarlatti owned one which would actually stroll across the keyboard and pick out passable subjects for fugue. But that was a Spanish cat of the Enlightenment. It appreciated counterpoint. Nowadays all cats appreciate are coloratura. Like the rest of the Public. (*He comes* D.S. *and addresses the Audience directly.*) This is now the very last hour of my life. You must understand me. Not forgive. I do not seek forgiveness. I was a good man, as the world calls good. What use was it to me? Goodness could not make me a good composer. Was Mozart good? Goodness is nothing in the furnace of art. (*Pause.*) On that dreadful night of the Manuscripts my life acquired a terrible and thrilling purpose. The blocking of God in one of his purest manifestations. I had the power. God needed Mozart to let himself into the world. And Mozart needed me to get him worldly advancement. So it would be a battle to the end—and Mozart was the battleground. (*Pause.*) One thing I knew of Him. He was a cunning Enemy. Witness the fact that in blocking Him in the world I was also given the satisfaction of obstructing a disliked human rival. I wonder which of you will refuse that chance if it is offered. (*He regards the Audience maliciously, taking off his dressing gown, cap and shawl.*) I felt the danger at once, as soon as I'd uttered my challenge. How would He answer? Would he strike me dead for my impiety? Don't laugh. I was not a sophisticate of the salons. I was a small town Catholic, full of dread! (*He puts on his powdered wig, and speaks again in his younger voice. We are back in the Eighteenth Century.*) The first thing that happened—barely one hour later—(*The doorbell sounds.* CONSTANZE *comes in followed by a helpless* VALET.) Suddenly Constanze was back. At ten o'clock at night! (*In surprise.*) Signora!

CONSTANZE. (*Stiffly.*) My husband is at a soirée of Baron Van Swieten. A concert of Sebastian Bach. He didn't think I would enjoy it.

SALIERI. I see. (*Curtly, to the goggling* VALET.) I'll ring if we require anything. Thank you. (*The* VALET *goes out. Slight pause.*)

CONSTANZE. (*Flatly.*) Where do we go, then?

SALIERI. What?

CONSTANZE. Do we do it in here? . . . Why not? (*She sits, still wearing her hat, in one of the little gilded upright chairs. Deliberately she loosens the strings of her bodice, so that one can just see the tops of her breasts, hitches up her silk skirts above the knees, so that one can also just see the flesh above the tops of the stockings, spreads her legs and regards him with an open stare. Speaking softly.*) Well? . . . Let's get on with it. (*For a second* SALIERI *returns the stare, then looks suddenly away.*)

SALIERI. (*Stiffly.*) Your manuscripts are there. Please take them and go. Now. At once. (*Pause.*)

CONSTANZE. You shit. (*She jumps up and snatches the portfolio.*)

SALIERI. *Via! Don't return!*

CONSTANZE. You rotten shit! (*Suddenly she runs at him—trying furiously to hit at his face. He grabs her arms, shakes her violently, and hurls her on the floor.*)

SALIERI. *Via! (She freezes, staring up at him in hate.)*
(Calling to Audience.) You see how it was! I would
have liked her — oh yes, just then more than ever! But
now I wanted nothing petty! . . . My quarrel wasn't
with Mozart — it was through him! Through him to God
who loved him so. *(Scornfully.) Amadeus!* . . . *[Am-*
adeus!] . . . *(*CONSTANZE *picks herself up and runs*
from the room. Pause. He calms himself, going to the
table and selecting a 'Nipple of Venus' to eat.) The next
day, when Katherina Cavalieri came for her lesson, I
made the same halting speech about 'coins of tenderness' — and I dubbed the girl *la Generosa.* I regret that
my invention in love, as in art, has always been limited.
Fortunately Katherina found it sufficient. She con-
sumed twenty 'Nipples of Venus' — kissed me with brandied breath — and slipped easily into my bed. *(*KATH-
ERINA *comes in languidly, half-undressed, as if from his*
bedroom. He embraces her, and helps slyly to adjust her
peignoir.) She remained there as my mistress for many
years behind my good wife's back — and I soon erased in
sweat the sense of his little body, the Creature's, preced-
ing me. *(The* GIRL *gives him a radiant smile, and ambles*
off.) So much for my vow of sexual virtue. *(Slight*
pause.) The same evening I went to the Palace and re-
signed from all my Committees to help the lot of poor
musicians. So much for my vow of social virtue. *(Light*
change.) Then I went to the Emperor and recommended
a man of no talent whatever to instruct the Princess
Elizabeth.

* * * *

The Palace of Schönbrunn.
The EMPEROR *stands before the vast fireplace, between*

the golden mirrors.

JOSEPH. Herr Sommer. A dull man, surely? What of Mozart?

SALIERI. Majesty, I cannot with a clear conscience recommend Mozart to teach Royalty. One hears too many stories.

JOSEPH. They may be just gossip.

SALIERI. One of them I regret relates to a protégée of my own. A very young singer.

JOSEPH. *Charmant!*

SALIERI. Not pleasant, Majesty, but true.

JOSEPH. I see . . . Let it be Herr Sommer, then. (*He walks down on to the main stage.*) I daresay he can't do much harm. To be frank, no one can do much harm musically to the Princess Elizabeth. (*He strolls away.* SALIERI *bows.* MOZART *enters from the other side,* D.S. *He wears a more natural-looking wig from now on: one indeed intended to represent his own hair of light chestnut, full and gathered at the back with ribbon.*)

SALIERI. (*To Audience.*) Mozart certainly did not suspect me. The Emperor announced the appointment in his usual way—

JOSEPH. (*Pausing.*) Well, there it is. (JOSEPH *goes off.*)

SALIERI. —and I commiserated with the loser. (MOZART *turns and stares bleakly out front.* SALIERI *shakes his hand.*)

MOZART. (*Bitterly.*) It's my own fault. My father always writes, I should be more obedient. *Know my place!* . . . He'll send me sixteen lectures when he hears of this! (MOZART *goes slowly up to the fortepiano. Lights lower.*)

SALIERI. (*To Audience, watching him.*) It was a most

serious loss as far as Mozart was concerned.

* * * *

Vienna, and Glimpses of Opera Houses.
The VENTICELLI *glide on.*

VENTICELLO 1. His list of pupils hardly moves.

VENTICELLO 2. Six at most.

VENTICELLO 1. And now a child to keep!

VENTICELLO 2. A boy.

SALIERI. Poor fellow. (*To Audience.*) I by contrast prospered. This is the extraordinary truth. If I had expected anger from God—none came. *None!* . . . Instead—incredibly—in '84 and '85 I came to be regarded as infinitely the superior composer. And this despite the fact that these were the two years in which Mozart wrote his best keyboard Concerti and his string Quartets. (*The* VENTICELLI *stand on either side of* SALIERI. MOZART *sits at the fortepiano.*)

VENTICELLO 1. Haydn calls the Quartets unsurpassed.

SALIERI. They were—but no one heard them.

VENTICELLO 2. Van Swieten calls the Concerti sublime.

SALIERI. They were, but no one noticed. (MOZART *plays and conducts from the keyboard. Faintly we hear the Rondo from the Piano Concerto in A major, K488.*) (*Over this.*) The Viennese greeted each unique Concerto with the squeals of pleasure they usually reserved for a new style of bonnet. Each was played once—then totally forgotten! I alone was empowered to recognize them fully for what they were: the most perfect things made by man in the whole of the 18th century . . . By contrast, my Operas were played everywhere and saluted by everyone! I composed my *Semiramide* for Munich.

VENTICELLO 1. Rapturously received!

VENTICELLO 2. People *faint* with pleasure! (*In the Light Box is seen the interior of a brilliantly coloured Opera House, and an Audience standing up, applauding vigorously.* SALIERI, *flanked by the* VENTICELLI, *turns* U.S. *and bows to it. The Concerto can scarcely be heard through the din.*)

SALIERI. I wrote a Comic opera for Vienna. *La Grotta di Trofonio.*

VENTICELLO 1. The talk of the City!

VENTICELLO 2. The Cafes are buzzing! (*Another Opera House interior is lit up. Another Audience claps vigorously. Again* SALIERI *bows to it.*)

SALIERI. I finally finished my tragic opera *Danaius*, and produced it in Paris.

VENTICELLO 1. Stupendous reception!

VENTICELLO 2. The plaudits shake the roof!

VENTICELLO 1. Your name sounds throughout the Empire!

VENTICELLO 2. Throughout all Europe! (*Yet another Opera House and another excited Audience.* SALIERI *bows a third time. Even the* VENTICELLI *now applaud him. The Concerto stops.* MOZART *rises from the keyboard and, whilst* SALIERI *speaks, crosses directly through the scene and leaves the stage.*)

SALIERI. (*To Audience.*) It was incomprehensible. Almost as if I were being pushed deliberately from triumph to triumph! . . . I filled my head with golden opinions—yes, and this house with golden furniture!

* * * *

SALIERI'S *Salon.*

The stage turns gold.

SERVANTS *come on carrying golden chairs upholstered in golden brocade. They place these all over the wooden floor.*

The VALET *appears — a little older — divests* SALIERI *of his sky-blue coat and clothes him instead in a frock coat of gold satin.*

The COOK *— also of course a little older — brings in a golden cake-stand piled with more elaborate cakes.*

SALIERI. My own taste was for plain things — but I *denied* it! . . . I grew confident. I grew resplendent. I gave salons and soirées, and worshipped the season round at the altar of success! (*He sits at ease in his salon drinking chocolate. The* VENTICELLI *sit with him, one on either side.*)

VENTICELLO 1. Mozart heard your comedy last night.

VENTICELLO 2. He spoke of it to the Princess Lichnowsky.

VENTICELLO 1. He said you should be made to clean up your own mess.

SALIERI. *Really?* What charmers these Salzburgers are!

VENTICELLO 2. People are outraged, by him.

VENTICELLO 1. He empties drawing-rooms. Now Van Swieten is angry with him.

SALIERI. Lord Fugue? I thought he was the Baron's little pet.

VENTICELLO 2. Mozart has asked leave to write an Italian opera.

SALIERI. (*Briskly aside, to Audience.*) Italian Opera! Threat! My kingdom!

VENTICELLO 1. And the Baron is scandalised.

SALIERI. But why? What's the theme of it? (*Van Swieten comes on quickly from* U.S.)

VAN SWIETEN. Figaro! . . . *The Marriage of Figaro!* That disgraceful play of Beaumarchais! (*At a discreet sign of dismissal from* SALIERI *the* VENTICELLI *slip away.* VAN SWIETEN *joins* SALIERI, *and sits on one of the gold chairs.*) (*To* SALIERI.) That's all he can find to waste his talent on: a vulgar farce. When I reproved him, he said I reminded him of his father! Noblemen lusting after chambermaids! Their wives dressing up in stupid disguises anyone could penetrate in a second! . . . Why set such rubbish . . . (MOZART *enters quickly from* U.S., *and* STRACK *from* D.R. *They join* SALIERI *and* VAN SWIETEN *sitting. A servant hands* MOZART *a cup of chocolate.*)

MOZART. Because I want to do a piece about real people, Baron! And I want to set it in a real place! A *boudoir!* — because that to me is the most exciting place on earth! Underclothes on the floor! Sheets still warm from a woman's body! Even a pisspot brimming under the bed!

VAN SWIETEN. (*Outraged.*) Mozart!

MOZART. I want life, Baron. Not boring legends!

STRACK. Herr Salieri's recent *Danaius* was a legend and that did not bore the French.

MOZART. It is impossible to bore the French — except with real life!

VAN SWIETEN. I had assumed, now that you had joined our Brotherhood of Masons, you would choose more elevated themes.

MOZART. (*Impatiently.*) Oh elevated! Elevated! . . . The only thing a man should elevate is his doodle.

VAN SWIETEN. You are provoking, sir! Has everything to be a joke with you?

MOZART. (*Desperate.*) Excuse language, Baron, but really! . . . How can we go on forever with these gods and heroes?

VAN SWIETEN. (*Passionately.*) Because they *go* on forever—that's why! They represent the eternal in us. Opera is here to ennoble us, Mozart—you and me just as well as the Emperor. It ís an aggrandising art! It celebrates the eternal in Man and ignores the ephemeral. The Goddess in Woman and not the laundress.

STRACK. Well said, sir. Exactly!

MOZART. (*Imitating his drawl.*) Oh well said, yes, well said! Exactly! (*To all of them.*) I don't understand you! You're all up on perches, but it doesn't hide your arseholes! You don't give a shit about gods and heroes! If you are honest—each one of you—which of you isn't more at home with his hairdresser than Hercules? Or Horatius? (*To* SALIERI.) Or your stupid *Danaius*, come to that! Or mine—*mine! Mitradate, King of Pontus!—Idomeneo, King of Crete!* All those anguished antiques! They're all bores! Bores, bores, bores! (*Suddenly he springs up and jumps on to a chair, like an orator. Declaring it.*) All serious operas written this century are boring! (*They turn and look at him in shocked amazement. A pause. He gives his little giggle, and then jumps up and down on the chair . . .*) Look at us! Four gaping mouths. What a perfect Quartet! I'd love to write it—just this second of time, this *now*, as you are! Herr Chamberlain thinking 'Impertinent Mozart: I must speak to the Emperor at once!' Herr Prefect thinking 'Ignorant Mozart: debasing opera with his vulgarity!' Herr Court Composer thinking 'German Mozart: what can he finally know about music?' And Herr Mozart himself, in the middle, thinking 'I'm just a good fellow. Why do they all disapprove of me?' (*Leaping off his chair. Excitedly, to* VAN SWIETEN.) That's why opera is important, Baron. Because it's realer than any play! A dramatic poet would have to put all those thoughts down one after another to represent this second of time. The composer can put them all down at once — and still make us hear each one of them. Astonishing device: a vocal quartet! (*More and more excited.*) . . . I tell you I want to write a finale lasting half an hour! A Quartet becoming a Quintet becoming a Sextet. On and on, wider and wider — all sounds multiplying and rising together — and the together making a sound entirely new! . . . I bet you that's how God hears the world. Millions of sounds ascending at once and mixing in His ear to become an unending music, unimaginable to us! (*To* SALIERI.) That's our job! That's our job, we composers: to combine the inner minds of him and him and him, and her and her — the thoughts of chambermaids and Court Composers — and turn the audience into God. (*Pause.* SALIERI *stares at him fascinated. Embarrassed,* MOZART *blows a raspberry and giggles.*) I'm sorry. I talk nonsense all day: it's incurable — ask Stanzerl. (*To* VAN SWIETEN.) My tongue is stupid. My heart isn't.

VAN SWIETEN. No. You're a good fellow under all your nonsense: I know that. He'll make a fine new Brother Mason, won't he, Salieri?

SALIERI. Better than I, Baron.

VAN SWIETEN. Just try, my friend, to be more serious with your gifts. (*He smiles, presses* MOZART's *hand, and goes.* SALIERI *rises.*)

SALIERI. *Buona fortuna, Mozart.*

MOZART. Grazie, Signore. (*Rounding on* STRACK.) Stop frowning, Herr Chamberlain. I'm a jackass. It's easy to be friends with a jackass: just shake his 'hoof'. (*He forms his hand into a 'hoof'. Warily* STRACK *takes it — then springs back as* MOZART *brays loudly like a donkey.*)

MOZART. *Hee-haw!* . . . Tell the Emperor the opera's

finished.

STRACK. Finished?

MOZART. Right here in my noodle. The rest's just scribbling. Goodbye.

STRACK. Good-day to you.

MOZART. He's going to be proud of me. You'll see. (*He gives his flourish of the hand and goes out, delighted with himself.*)

STRACK. That young man really is . . .

SALIERI. (*Blandly.*) Very lively.

STRACK. (*Exploding.*) Intolerable! . . . *Intolerable!* (STRACK *freezes in a posture of indignation.*)

SALIERI. (*To Audience.*) How could I stop it? . . . How could I block this opera of Figaro? . . . Incredible to hear, within six weeks, the creature had finished the entire score. (ROSENBERG *bustles in.*)

ROSENBERG. Figaro is complete! The first performance will be on May the first!

SALIERI. So soon?

ROSENBERG. There's no way we can stop it! (*A slight pause.*)

SALIERI. (*Slyly.*) I have an idea. *Una piccola idea!*

ROSENBERG. What?

SALIERI. *Mi ha detto che un balletto nel terzo atto?*

ROSENBERG. (*Puzzled.*) *Sì.*

STRACK. What does he say?

SALIERI. *E dimmi—non è vero che l'Imperatore ha probito il balletto nelle sue opere?*

ROSENBERG. (*Realising.*) *Uno balletto* . . . Ah!

SALIERI. *Precisamente.*

ROSENBERG. Oh, *capisco! Ma che meraviglia! Perfetto!* (*He laughs in delight.*) *Veramente ingegnoso!*

STRACK. (*Irritated.*) What is it? What is he suggesting?

SALIERI. See him at the theatre.

ROSENBERG. Of course. Immediately. I'd forgotten. You are brilliant, Court Composer.

SALIERI. I? . . . I have said nothing. (*He moves away* U.S. *The light begins to change, dimming down.*)

STRACK. (*Very cross.*) I must tell you that I resent this extremely. Mozart is right in some things. There is far too much Italian *chittero-chattero* at this Court! Now please to inform me at once, what was just said?

ROSENBERG. (*Lightly.*) *Pazienza,* my dear Chamberlain. *Pazienza.* Just wait and see! (*From* U.S. SALIERI *beckons to* STRACK. *Baffled and cross, the* CHAMBERLAIN *joins him. They watch together, unseen. The light dims further.*)

***

An Unlit Theatre.

In the background a projection of lamps glowing faintly in the darkened auditorium. ROSENBERG *sits on one of the gold chairs,* C.

MOZART *comes in quickly from the* L., *wearing another bright coat, and carrying the score of* Figaro. *He crosses to the fortepiano.*

ROSENBERG. Mozart . . . *Mozart!*

MOZART. Yes, Herr Director.

ROSENBERG. (*Agreeably.*) A word with you, please. Right away.

MOZART. Certainly. What is it?

ROSENBERG. I would like to see your score of *Figaro.*

MOZART. Oh yes. Why?

ROSENBERG. Just bring it here to me. (*Unmoving.*) Into my hand, please. (MOZART *hands it to him puzzled.*

ROSENBERG *turns the pages.*) Now tell me: did you not know that His Majesty has expressly forbidden ballet in his operas?

MOZART. Ballet?

ROSENBERG. Such as occurs in your third act.

MOZART. That is not a ballet, Herr Director. That is a dance at Figaro's wedding.

ROSENBERG. Exactly. A dance.

MOZART. (*Trying to control himself.*) But, the Emperor doesn't mean to prohibit dancing when it's part of the story. He made that law to prevent insertions of stupid ballet like in French operas, and quite right too.

ROSENBERG. (*Raising his voice.*) It is not for you, Herr Mozart, to interpret the Emperor's edicts. Merely to obey them. (*He seizes the offending pages between his fingers.*)

MOZART. What are you doing? . . . What are you doing, Excellency?

ROSENBERG. Taking out what should never have been put in. (*In a terrible silence* ROSENBERG *tears out the pages,* MOZART *watches in disbelief.* U.S. SALIERI *and* STRACK *look on together from the dimness.*) Now, sir, perhaps in future you will obey Imperial commands. (*He tears out some more pages.*)

MOZART. But . . . But—if all that goes—there'll be a hole right at the climax of the story! . . . (*Crying out suddenly.*) Salieri! This is Salieri's idea!

ROSENBERG. Don't be absurd.

SALIERI. (*To Audience.*) How did he think of that? Nothing I had ever done could possibly make him think of that on his own. Had God given him the idea?!

MOZART. It's a conspiracy. I can smell it. I can smell it!

ROSENBERG. Control yourself!

MOZART. (*Howling.*) *But what do you expect me to do?* The first performance is two days off!

ROSENBERG. Write it over. That's your forte, is it not? — writing at speed.

MOZART. Not when the music's *perfect!* Not when it's absolutely perfect as it is! . . . (*Wildly.*) I shall appeal to the Emperor! I'll go to him myself! I'll hold a rehearsal especially for him.

ROSENBERG. The Emperor does not attend rehearsals.

MOZART. He'll attend this one. Make no mistake — he'll come to this one! Then he'll deal with *you!*

ROSENBERG. The issue is simple. Write your Act again today — or withdraw the opera. That's final. (*Pause. He hands back the mutilated score to its composer. MOZART is shaking.*)

MOZART. You shit-pot. (ROSENBERG *turns and walks imperturbably away from him.*) Woppy, foppy, wet-arsed, Italian-loving, shit-pot! (*Serenely,* ROSENBERG *leaves the stage.*) (*Screeching after him.*) Count Orsini-Rosenshit! . . . Rosenhole! . . . Rosenbugger! . . . I'll hold a rehearsal! You'll see! The Emperor will come! You'll see! You'll see! . . . *You'll see!!* (*He throws down his score in a storm of hysterical rage.* U.S. *in the dimness* STRACK *goes out, and* SALIERI *ventures down towards the shrieking little man.* MOZART *suddenly becomes aware of him. He turns, his hand shooting out in an involuntary gesture of accusation.*) (*To* SALIERI.) I am *forbidden!* . . . I am — forbidden! . . . But of course you know already!

SALIERI. (*Quietly.*) Know what? (MOZART *flings away from him.*)

MOZART. (*Bitterly.*) No matter!

SALIERI. (*Always blandly.*) Mozart, permit me. If you wish, I will speak to the Emperor myself. Ask him to attend a rehearsal.

MOZART. (*Amazed.*) You wouldn't.

SALIERI. I cannot promise he will come — but I can try.

MOZART. Sir! —

SALIERI. Good day. (*He puts up his hands, barring further intimacy.* MOZART *retreats to the fortepiano.*) (*To Audience.*) Needless to say I did nothing whatever in the matter. Yet — to my total stupefaction — (STRACK *and* ROSENBERG *hurry on* D.S.) — in the middle of the last rehearsal of *Figaro* next day . . . (*The* EMPEROR JOSEPH *comes on from* U.S.)

JOSEPH. (*Cheerfully.*) Fêtes and fireworks! Fetes and fireworks! Gentlemen, good afternoon!

* * * *

The Theatre.

SALIERI. (*To Audience.*) Entirely against his usual practice, the Emperor appeared! (STRACK *and* ROSENBERG *look at each other in consternation.* JOSEPH *seats himself excitedly on one of the gold chairs, facing out front. As with the premiere of* Seraglio *seen in Act I, he watches the Audience as if it were the opera.*)

JOSEPH. I can't wait for this, Mozart, I assure you! *Je prevois des merveilles!*

MOZART. (*Bowing fervently.*) Majesty! (*The* COURTIERS *sit also:* STRACK *on his right-hand side,* ROSENBERG *on his left.* SALIERI *also sits, near the keyboard.*)

SALIERI. (*To Audience.*) What did this mean? Was this proof God had finally decided to defend Mozart against me? Was He engaging with me at last? (MOZART *passes behind* SALIERI.)

MOZART. (*Earnestly, sotto voce.*) I am so grateful to you, I cannot express it!

SALIERI. (*Aside, to him.*) Hush. Say nothing. (*Mozart goes on quickly to the fortepiano and sits at it.*) (*To Audience.*) One thing about the event certainly seemed more than coincidence. (*Music sounds faintly: the end of the third act of* Figaro, *just before the dance music starts.*) Strangely, His Majesty had arrived at precisely the moment when the dancers would have begun, (*Pause.*) had not they and their music been entirely cut. (*The music stops abruptly.*) He and all of us watched the action as it proceeded in total silence. (*Flanked by his* COURTIERS, *the* EMPEROR *stares out front, following with his eyes what is obviously a silent pantomime. His face expresses bewilderment.* ROSENBERG *watches his* SOVEREIGN *anxiously. Finally the* MONARCH *speaks.*)

JOSEPH. I don't understand. Is it modern?

MOZART. (*Jumping up nervously from the keyboard.*) No, Majesty.

JOSEPH. Then what?

MOZART. The Herr Director has removed a dance that would have occurred at this point.

JOSEPH. (*To* ROSENBERG.) Why was this done?

ROSENBERG. It's your own regulation, Sire. No ballet in your Opera.

MOZART. Majesty, this is not a ballet. It is part of a wedding feast: entirely necessary for the story.

JOSEPH. Well, it certainly looks very odd the way it is. I can't say I like it.

MOZART. Nor do I, Majesty.

JOSEPH. Do you like it, Rosenberg?

ROSENBERG. It's not a question of liking, Majesty. Your own Law decrees it.

JOSEPH. Yes. All the same, this is nonsense. Look at

them: they're like waxworks up there.

ROSENBERG. Well, not exactly, Majesty.

JOSEPH. I don't like waxworks.

MOZART. Nor do I, Majesty.

JOSEPH. Well, who would? What do you say, Salieri?

SALIERI. Italians are fond of waxworks, Majesty. (*Pause.*) Our religion is largely based upon them.

JOSEPH. You are *cattivo* again, Court Composer.

STRACK. (*Intervening creamily.*) Your Majesty, Count Rosenberg is very worried that if this music is put back it will create the most unfortunate precedent. One will have thereafter to endure hours of dancing in opera.

JOSEPH. (*Dryly.*) I think we can guard against that, you know, Chamberlain. I really think we can guard against hours of dancing. (*To* ROSENBERG.) Please restore Herr Mozart's music.

ROSENBERG. But Majesty, I must insist—

JOSEPH. (*With a touch of anger.*) You will oblige me, Rosenberg! I wish to hear Mozart's music. Do you understand me?

ROSENBERG. Yes, Majesty. (MOZART *explodes with joy, jumps over a chair and throws himself at* JOSEPH's *feet.*)

MOZART. Oh God, I thank your Majesty! (*He kisses the* EMEROR's *hand extravagantly, as at their first meeting.*) Oh thank you—thank you—thank you Sire, forever!

JOSEPH. (*Withdrawing his hand.*) Yes, yes—very good. A little less enthusiasm, I beg you!

MOZART. (*Abashed.*) Excuse me. (*The* EMPEROR *rises. All follow suit.*)

JOSEPH. Well. *There it is!*

* * * *

The First Performance of Figaro.

*The Theater glows with light for the first performance
of* Figaro. COURTIERS *and* CITIZENS *come in swiftly.*

The EMPEROR *and his* COURT *resume their seats and the*
OTHERS *quickly take theirs. In the front row we
note* KATHERINA CAVALIERI, *all plumes and sequins,
and Kapellmeister* BONNO — *older than ever. Behind
them sit* CONSTANZE *and the* VENTICELLI. *All of
them stare out at the Audience as if it were the
opera they have come to see:* PEOPLE OF FASHION
down front; POORER PEOPLE *crowded into the Light
Box* U.S.

SALIERI *crosses as he speaks to where two chairs have
been placed side by side apart from the rest, on the
L., to form his box. On the chair U.S. sits his good
wife* TERESA — *more statuesque than ever.*

SALIERI. (*To Audience.*) And so *Figaro* was produced
in spite of all my efforts. I sat in my box and watched it
happen. A conspicuous defeat for me. And yet I was
strangely excited. (*Faintly we hear Figaro singing the
tune of 'Non piu andrai'. The stage* AUDIENCE *is obviously delighted: they smile out front as they watch the
invisible action.*) My March! My poor March of Welcome — now set to enchant the world forever! (*It fades.
Applause. The* EMPEROR *rises, and with him the Audience, to denote an Intermission.* JOSEPH *greets* KATHER-
INA *and* BONNO. ROSENBERG *and* STRACK *go to* SALIERI'S
box.)

ROSENBERG. (*To* SALIERI.) Almost in your style, that
last bit. But more vulgar of course. Far more obvious
than you would ever be.

SALIERI. (*Drawling.*) Exactly! (*A bell rings for the
end of the Intermission. The* EMPEROR *returns quickly*

to his seat. The AUDIENCE *sits. A pause. All look out front, unmoving.*)

SALIERI. (*Raptly and quietly: to Audience.*) Trembling, I heard the second act. (*Pause.*) The restored third act. (*Pause.*) The astounding fourth. What shall I say to you who will one day hear this last act for yourselves? You will — because whatever else shall pass away, this must remain. (*Faintly we hear the solemn closing ensemble from act four of* Figaro, '*Ah! Tutti contenti. Saremo cosi'.*) (*Over this.*) The scene was night in a summer garden. Pinprick stars gleamed down on shaking summerhouses. Plotters glided behind pasteboard hedges. I saw a woman, dressed in her maid's clothes, hear her husband utter the first tender words he has offered her in years only because he thinks she is someone else. Could one catch a realer moment? And how, except in a net of pure artifice? The disguises of opera had been invented for Mozart. (*He can barely look out at the 'stage'.*) The final reconciliation melted sight. (*Pause.*) Through my tears I saw the Emperor — yawn. (JOSEPH *yawns. The music fades. There is scant applause.* JOSEPH *rises and the* COURTIERS *follow suit.* MOZART *bows.*)

JOSEPH. (*Coolly.*) Most ingenious, Mozart. You are coming along nicely . . . I do think we must omit encores in future. It really makes things far too long. Make a note, Rosenberg.

ROSENBERG. Majesty. (MOZART *lowers his head, crushed.*)

JOSEPH. Gentlemen, good night to you. Strack, attend me. (JOSEPH *goes out, with* STRACK. *Director* ROSENBERG *gives* MOZART *one triumphant look and follows.* SALIERI *nods to his* WIFE *who leaves with the* AUDIENCE. *Only* CONSTANZE *lingers for a second, then she too goes.*

A pause. MOZART *and* SALIERI *are left alone:* SALIERI *deeply shaken by the opera.* MOZART *deeply upset by its reception. He crosses and sits next to* SALIERI.)

MOZART. (*Low.*) Herr Salieri.

SALIERI. Yes?

MOZART. What do you think? Do you think I am coming along nicely?

SALIERI. (*Moved.*) I think the piece is . . . extraordinary. I think it is . . . *marvellous.* Yes. (*Pause.* MOZART *turns to him.*)

MOZART. I'll tell you what it is. It's the best opera yet written. That's what it is. And only I could have done it. No one else living! (SALIERI *turns his head swiftly, as if he has been slapped.* MOZART *rises and walks away. The light changes. The* VENTICELLI *rush on.* SALIERI *and* MOZART *both freeze.*)

VENTICELLO 1. Rosenberg is furious.

VENTICELLO 2. He'll never forgive Mozart.

VENTICELLO 1. He'll do anything to get back at him!

SALIERI. (*Rising: to Audience.*) So it wasn't hard to get the piece cancelled. I saw to it through the person of the resentful Director that in the entire year *Figaro* was played only *nine times!* . . . My defeat finally turned into a Victory. And God's response to my challenge remained as inscrutable as ever . . . Was He taking any notice of me *at all*? . . . (MOZART *breaks his freeze and comes* D.S.)

MOZART. *Withdrawn!* Absolutely no plans for its revival!

SALIERI. I commiserate with you, my friend. But if the Public does not like one's work, one has to accept the fact gracefully. (*Aside, to Audience.*) And certainly they didn't.

VENTICELLO 1. (*Complaining.*) It's too complicated!

VENTICELLO 2. (*Complaining.*) Too tiresome!

VENTICELLO 1. All those weird harmonies!

VENTICELLO 2. And never a good bang at the end of songs so you know when to clap! (*The* VENTICELLI *go off.*)

SALIERI. (*To Audience.*) Obviously I would not need to plot too hard against his operas in future. The Viennese could be relied upon to destroy those for me. I must concentrate on the man. I decided to see him as much as possible: to learn everything I could of his weaknesses.

* * * *

The Waldstädten Library.
SERVANTS *again bring on the wing-chair.*

MOZART. I'll go to England. England loves music. That's the answer!

SALIERI. (*To Audience.*) We were yet again in the Library of the Baroness Waldstädten: that room fated to be the scene of ghastly encounters between us. Again, too, the compensating *crema al mascarpone.* (*He sits in the chair and eats greedily.*)

MOZART. I was there when I was a boy. They absolutely adored me. I had more kisses than you've had cakes! . . . When I was a child, people loved me.

SALIERI. Perhaps they will again. Why don't you go to London and try?

MOZART. Because I have a wife and child and no money. I wrote to Papa to take the boy off my hands just for a few months so I could go—and he refused! . . . In the end everyone betrays you, even the man you think loves you most. He's a bitter man, of course. After he'd finished showing me off around Europe he never went anywhere himself. He just stayed up in Salzburg year after year, kissing the ring of the Fartsbishop and lecturing me! . . . (*Confidentially.*) The real thing is, you see, he's jealous. Under everything he's jealous of me! He'll never forgive me for being cleverer than he is. (*He leans excitedly over* SALIERI's *chair like a naughty child.*) I'll tell you a secret. Leopold Mozart is just a jealous, dried up old turd . . . And I actually detest him. (*He giggles guitily. The* VENTICELLI *appear quickly, and address* SALIERI, *as* MOZART *freezes.*)

VENTICELLO 1. (*Solemnly.*) Leopold Mozart—

VENTICELLO 2. (*Solemnly.*) Leopold Mozart—

VENTICELLO 1 & Venticello 2. *Leopold Mozart is dead!* (*They go off.* MOZART *recoils. A long pause.*)

SALIERI. Do not despair. Death is inevitable, my friend.

MOZART. (*Desperately.*) How will I go now?

SALIERI. What do you mean?

MOZART. In the world. There's no one else. No one who understands the wickedness around. *I can't see it!* . . . He watched for me all my life—and I betrayed him.

SALIERI. No!

MOZART. I talked against him.

SALIERI. No!

MOZART. (*Distressed.*) I married where he begged me not. I left him alone. I danced and played billiards and fooled about, and he sat by himself night after night in an empty house, and no woman to care for him . . . (SALIERI *rises in concern.*)

SALIERI. Wolfgang. My dear Wolfgang. Don't accuse yourself! . . . Lean upon me, if you care to . . . Lean upon me. (SALIERI *opens his arms in a wide gesture of paternal benevolence.* MOZART *approaches, and is almost tempted to surrender to the embrace. But at the last moment he avoids it, and breaks away down front, to fall on his knees.*)

MOZART. *Papa!*

SALIERI. (*To Audience.*) So rose the Ghost Father in *Don Giovanni!*

* * * *

The two grim chords which open the Overture to Don Giovanni *sound through the theatre.* MOZART *seems to quail under them, as he stares out front. On the backdrop in the Light Box appears the silhouette of a giant black figure, in cloak and tricorne hat. It extends its arms, menacingly and engulfingly, towards its begetter.*

SALIERI. A Father more accusing than any in opera. So rose the figure of a Guilty Libertine, cast into Hell! . . . I looked on astounded as from his ordinary life he made his art. We were both ordinary men, he and I. Yet he from the ordinary created legends — and I from legends created only the ordinary. (*The figure fades.* SALIERI *stands over the kneeling* MOZART.) Could I not have stopped my war? Shown him some pity? Oh yes, my friends, at any time — if He above had shown me one drop of it! Every day I set to work I prayed — I still prayed, you understand — 'Make this one good in my ears! Just this one! *One!*' But would He ever? . . . I heard my music calmed in convention — not one breath of spirit to lift it off the shallows. And I heard *his* — (*We hear the exquisite strains of the Terzetto 'Soave il Vento' from* Cosi Fan Tutte.) the spirit singing through it unstoppable to my ears alone! I heard his comedy of the seduction of two sisters, *Cosi Fan Tutte: Thus do all women.* Aloysia and Constanze immortalised — two average girls turned into divinities: their sounds of surrender sweeter than the psalms in Heaven. (*To God, in anguish.*) 'Grant this to me! Grant this to me! . . .' (*As God.*) 'No, no, no, I do not need you, Salieri! I have Mozart! Better for you to be silent!' *Hahahahaha!* (*The music cuts off.*) The Creature's dreadful giggle was the laughter of God! . . . I had to end it. But how? There was only one way. *Starvation.* Starve out the God. Reduce the man to destitution.

* * * *

Vienna and the Palace of Schönbrunn.

SALIERI. (*To* MOZART.) How do you fare today?

MOZART. Badly. I have no money, and no prospect of any.

SALIERI. It would not be too hard, surely. (*Lights up on The Palace of Schönbrunn. The* EMPEROR *stands in the Light Box, in his golden space.*)

JOSEPH. We must find him a Post.

SALIERI. (*To Audience.*) One danger! The Emperor. (SALIERI GOES U.S. *to* JOSEPH.) There's nothing available, Majesty.

JOSEPH. There's Chamber Composer now that Gluck is dead.

SALIERI. (*Shocked.*) Mozart to follow Gluck?

JOSEPH. I won't have him say I drove him away. You know what a tongue he has.

SALIERI. Then grant him Gluck's post, Majesty, but

not his salary. That would be wrong.

JOSEPH. Gluck got 2000 florins a year. What should Mozart get?

SALIERI. 200. Light payment, yes, but for light duties.

JOSEPH. Perfectly fair. I'm obliged to you, Court Composer.

SALIERI. (*Bowing.*) Majesty. (*Lights down a little on* JOSEPH, *who still stands there.* SALIERI *returns to* MOZART.) (*To Audience.*) Easily done. Like many men obsessed with being thought generous, the Emperor Joseph was quite essentially stingy. (MOZART *kneels before the* EMPEROR.)

JOSEPH. Herr Mozart. Vous nous faites honneur! . . . (*Lights.* MOZART *turns and walks* D.S.)

MOZART. It's a damned insult! Not enough to keep a mouse in cheese for a week!

SALIERI. Regard it as a token, *caro* Herr.

MOZART. When I was young they gave me snuff boxes. Now it's tokens! And for what? Pom-pom, for fireworks! Twang-twang for Contredanzes!

SALIERI. I'm sorry it's made you angry. I'd not have suggested it if I'd known you'd be distressed.

MOZART. You suggested it?

SALIERI. I regret I was not able to do more.

MOZART. Oh . . . forgive me! You're a good man! I see that now! You're a truly kind man — and I'm a monstrous fool! (*He grasps* SALIERI's *hand.*)

SALIERI. No, please . . .

MOZART. You make me ashamed . . . You excellent man!

SALIERI. No, no, no, no, no, — s'il vous plait. A little less enthusiasm I beg you! (MOZART *laughs delightedly at this imitation of the* EMPEROR. SALIERI *joins in.* MOZART *suddenly doubles over with stomach cramps. He groans.*) *Wolfgang!* What is it?

MOZART. I get cramps sometimes in my stomach.

SALIERI. I'm sorry.

MOZART. Excuse me . . . it's nothing really.

SALIERI. I will see you soon again?

MOZART. Of course.

SALIERI. Why not visit me?

MOZART. I will . . . I promise!

SALIERI. Bene.

MOZART. Bene.

SALIERI. My friend. My new friend. (MOZART *giggles with pleasure and goes off. A pause.*) (*To Audience.*) Now if ever was the moment for God to crush me. I waited—and do you know what happened? I had just ruined Mozart's career at Court: God rewarded me by granting my dearest wish! (*The* VENTICELLI *come on.*)

VENTICELLO 1. Kapellmeister Bonno.

VENTICELLO 2. Kapellmeister Bonno.

VENTICELLO 1 & VENTICELLO 2. *Kapellmeister Bonno is dead!* (SALIERI *opens his mouth in surprise.*)

VENTICELLO 1. You are appointed—

VENTICELLO 2. By Royal Decree—

VENTICELLO 1. To fill his place. (*Lights full up on the* EMPEROR *at the back. He is flanked by* STRACK *and* ORSINI-ROSENBERG, *standing like icons as at their first appearance.*)

JOSEPH. (*Formally as* SALIERI *turns and bows to him.*) First Royal and Imperial Kapellmeister to our Court. (*The* VENTICELLI *applaud.*)

VENTICELLO 1. Bravo.

VENTICELLO 2. Bravo.

ROSENBERG. Eviva, Salieri!

STRACK. Well done, Salieri!

JOSEPH. (*Warmly.*) Dear Salieri—There it is! (*The lights go down on Schönbrunn. In the dark the* EMPEROR *and his Court leave the stage for the last time.* SALIERI *turns round, alarmed.*)

[SALIERI.] (*To Audience.*) I was now truly alarmed. How long would I go unpunished?

VENTICELLO 1 & VENTICELLO 2. Congratulations, Sir!

VENTICELLO 1. Mozart looks appalling.

VENTICELLO 2. It must be galling of course.

VENTICELLO 1. I hear he's dosing himself constantly with medicine.

SALIERI. For what?

VENTICELLO 2. Envy, I imagine!

VENTICELLO 1. I hear there's another child on the way . . .

VENTICELLO 2. There is. I've seen the mother.

* * * *

The Prater.

Fresh green trees appear on the backdrop. The light changes to yellow, turning the blue surround into a rich verdant green.

MOZART *ar 1* CONSTANZE *enter arm-in-arm. She is palpably pregnant and wears a poor coat and bonnet; his clothes are poorer too.* SALIERI *promenades with the* VENTICELLI.)

SALIERI. I met him next in the Prater.

MOZART. (*To* SALIERI.) Congratulations, sir!

SALIERI. I thank you. And to you both! (*To Audience.*) Clearly there was a change for the worse. His eyes gleamed, oddly, like a dog's when the light catches. (*To* MOZART.) I hear you are not well, my friend. (*He acknowledges* CONSTANZE, *who curtseys to him.*)

MOZART. I'm not. My pains stay with me.

SALIERI. How wretched. What can they be?

MOZART. Also, I sleep badly . . . I have . . . bad dreams.

CONSTANZE. (*Warningly.*) Wolferl!

SALIERI. Dreams?

MOZART. Always the same one . . . A figure comes to me cloaked in grey—doing this. (*He beckons slowly.*) It has no face. Just grey—like a mask . . . (*He giggles nervously.*) What can it mean, do you think?

SALIERI. Surely you do not believe in dreams?

MOZART. No, of course not—really!

SALIERI. Surely *you* do not, Madame?

CONSTANZE. I never dream, sir. Things are unpleasant enough to me, awake. (SALIERI *bows.*)

MOZART. It's all fancy, of course!

CONSTANZE. If Wolfgang had proper work he might dream less, First Kapellmeister.

MOZART. (*Embarrassed, taking her arm.*) Stanzi, please! . . . Excuse us, sir. Come, dearest. We are well enough, thank you! (*Husband and wife go off.*)

VENTICELLO 1. He's growing freakish.

VENTICELLO 2. No question.

VENTICELLO 1. Grey figures with masked faces!

SALIERI. (*Looking after him.*) He broods on his father too much, I fancy. Also his circumstances make him anxious.

VENTICELLO 1. They've moved house again.

VENTICELLO 2. To the Rauhensteingasse. Number 970.

VENTICELLO 1. They must be desperate.

VENTICELLO 2. It's a real slum.

SALIERI. Does he earn any money at all, apart from his Post?

VENTICELLO 1. Nothing whatever.

VENTICELLO 2. I hear he's starting to beg.

VENTICELLO 1. They say he's written letters to twenty

Brother Masons.

SALIERI. Really?

VENTICELLO 2. And they're giving him money.

SALIERI. (*To Audience.*) Of course! They *would!* . . .
I had *forgotten* the Masons! *Naturally* they would relieve him — *how stupid of me!* . . . There could be no
finally starving him with the Masons there to help! As
long as he asked they would keep supplying his wants . . .
How could I stop it? [And quickly!] . . .

VENTICELLO 1. Lord Fugue is most displeased with
him!

SALIERI. *Is* he?

* * * *

A Masonic Lodge.

*A huge golden emblem descends, encrusted with Ma-
sonic symbols. Enter* VAN SWIETEN. *He is wearing
the ritual apron apron over his sober clothes. At the
same time* MOZART *enters from the* L. *He too wears
the apron. The two men clasp hands in fraternal
greeting.*

VAN SWIETEN. (*Gravely.*) This is not good, Brother.
The Lodge was not created for you to beg from.

MOZART. What else can I do?

VAN SWIETEN. Give concerts, as you used to do.

MOZART. I have no subscribers left, Baron. I am no
longer fashionable.

VAN SWIETEN. I am not surprised. You write tasteless
comedies which give offence. I warned you, often
enough.

MOZART. (*Humbly.*) You did. I admit it. (*He holds
his stomach in pain.*)

VAN SWIETEN. I will send you some Fugues of Bach

tomorrow. You can arrange those for my Sunday concert. You shall have a small fee.

MOZART. Thank you, Baron. (VAN SWIETEN *nods and goes out.* SALIERI *steps forward. He again wears the Masonic apron.*) (*Shouting after* VAN SWIETEN.) I cannot live by arranging Bach!

SALIERI. (*Sarcastically.*) A generous fellow.

MOZART. All the same, I'll have to do it. If he were to turn the Lodge against me, I'd be finished.

SALIERI. Absolutely true.

MOZART. My Brother Masons virtually keep me now . . . Never mind. I'll manage: you'll see! Things are looking up already. I've had a marvellous proposal from Schickaneder. He's a new Member of this Lodge.

SALIERI. Schickaneder? The actor?

MOZART. Yes. He owns a theatre in the suburbs.

SALIERI. Well, more of a Music Hall, surely?

MOZART. Yes . . . He wants me to write him a Vaudeville—something for ordinary German people. Isn't that a wonderful idea? . . . He's offered me half the receipts when we open.

SALIERI. Nothing in advance?

MOZART. He said he couldn't afford anything. I know it's not much of an offer. But a popular piece about Brotherly Love could celebrate everything we believe as Masons!

SALIERI. It certainly could! . . . Why don't you put the Masons *into* it?

MOZART. Into an opera? . . . I couldn't! (SALIERI *laughs, to indicate that he was simply making a joke.*) All the same—what an idea! . . .

SALIERI. (*Earnestly.*) Our rituals are secret, Wolfgang.

MOZART. I needn't copy them exactly. I could adapt them a little.

SALIERI. Well . . . It would certainly be in a great cause.

MOZART. Brotherly Love!

SALIERI. Brotherly Love! (*They both turn and look solemnly at the great golden emblem hanging at their backs.*) (*Warmly.*) Try it and see. Take courage, Wolfgang. It's a glorious idea.

MOZART. It is, isn't it? It *really is!*

SALIERI. Of course say nothing till it's done.

MOZART. Not a word.

SALIERI. (*Making a sign: closed fist.*) Secret!

MOZART. (*Making a similar sign.*) Secret!

SALIERI. Good. (*He steps out of the scene D.s.*) (*To Audience.*) And if that didn't finish him off with the Masons — nothing would! (*The gold emblem withdraws. We hear the merry dance of Monastatos and the hypnotised slaves from 'The Magic Flute':* "Das Klinget, so herrlich Das Klinget so schön!" *To the tinkling of the glockenspiel Servants bring in a long plain table loaded with manuscripts and bottles. It also bears a plain upturned stool. They place this in the wooden area head-on to the Audience. At the same time* CONSTANZE *appears wearily from the back, and enters this apartment: the Rauhensteingasse. She wears a stuffed apron, indicating the advanced state of her pregnancy. Simultaneously* U.L., *two other Servants have placed the little gilded table bearing a loaded cake-stand and three of the gilded chairs from* SALIERI'S *resplendent Salon. We now have in view the two contrasting apartments. As soon as the emblem withdraws, the* VENTICELLI *appear to* SALIERI.)

* * * *

MOZART'S *Apartment:* SALIERI'S *Apartment*

VENTICELLO 1. Mozart is delighted with himself!

VENTICELLO 2. He's writing a secret opera!

VENTICELLO 1. (*Crossly.*) And won't tell anyone its theme.

VENTICELLO 2. It's really too tiresome! (*The* VENTICELLI *go off.*)

SALIERI. He told *me*. He told me everything! . . . Initiation ceremonies. Ceremonies with blindfolds. All rituals copied from the Masons! . . . He sat at home preparing his own destruction. A home where life grew daily more grim. (*He goes* U.S. *and sits on one of his gilded chairs, devouring a cake.* MOZART *also sits at his table, wrapped in a blanket, and starts to write music. Opposite him* CONSTANZE *sits on a stool, wrapped in a shawl.*)

CONSTANZE. I'm cold . . . I'm cold all day . . . Hardly surprising since we have no firewood.

MOZART. Papa was right. We end exactly as he said. Beggars.

CONSTANZE. It's all his fault.

MOZART. Papa's?

CONSTANZE. He kept you a baby all your life.

MOZART. I don't understand . . . You always loved Papa.

CONSTANZE. Did I?

MOZART. You adored him. You told me so often. (*Slight pause.*)

CONSTANZE. (*Flatly.*) I hated him.

MOZART. What?

CONSTANZE. And he hated me.

MOZART. That's absurd. He loved us both very much. You're being extremely silly now.

CONSTANZE. Am I?

MOZART. (*Airily.*) Yes, you are, little-wife-of-my-heart!

CONSTANZE. Do you remember the fire we had last night, because it was so cold you couldn't even get the ink wet? You said, "What a blaze" — remember? "What a blaze! All those old papers going up!" Well, my dear, those old papers were just all your Father's letters, that's all — every one he wrote since the day we married.

MOZART. *What?*

CONSTANZE. Every one! All the letters about what a ninny I am — what a bad housekeeper I am! Every one!

MOZART. (*Crying out.*) Stanzi!

CONSTANZE. *Shit on him! . . . Shit on him!*

MOZART. *You bitch!*

CONSTANZE. (*Savagely.*) At least it kept us warm! What else will do that? Perhaps we should dance! You love to dance, Wolferl — let's dance! Dance to keep warm! (*Grandly.*) Write me a contredanze, Mozart! It's your job to write dances, isn't it? (*Hysterical, she starts dancing roughly round the room like a demented peasant to the tune of* 'Non più andrai!' *Singing wildly.*) *Non piu andrai, farfallone amoroso — Notte é giorno d'intorno girando!*

MOZART. (*Shrieking.*) *Stop it! Stop it!* (*He seizes her.*) Stanzi-marini! Marini-bini! Don't, please. Please, please, please I beg you . . . Look there's a kiss! Where's it coming from? Right out of that corner! There's another one — all wet, all sloppy wet coming straight to *you!* Kiss — kiss — kiss! (*She pushes him away.* CONSTANZE *dances.* MOZART *catches her. She pushes him away.*)

CONSTANZE. Get off! (*Pause.*)

MOZART. I'm frightened, Stanzi. Something awful's happening to me.

CONSTANZE. I can't bear it. I can't bear much more of this.

MOZART. And the Figure's like this now — (*Beckoning faster.*) "Here! Come here! Here!" Its face still masked — invisible! It becomes realer and realer to me!

CONSTANZE. Stop it, for God's sake! . . . Stop! . . . It's me who's frightened . . . *Me!* . . . You frighten me . . . If you go on like this I'll leave you. I swear it.

MOZART. (*Shocked.*) Stanzi!

CONSTANZE. I mean it . . . I do . . . (*She puts her hand to her stomach, as if in pain.*)

MOZART. I'm sorry . . . Oh God, I'm sorry . . . I'm sorry, I'm sorry, I'm sorry! . . . Come here to me, little wife of my heart! Come . . . Come . . . (*He kneels and coaxes her to him. She comes half-reluctantly, half-willingly.*) Who am I? . . . Quick: tell me. Hold me and tell who I am.

CONSTANZE. Pussy-wussy.

MOZART. Who else?

CONSTANZE. Miaowy-powy.

MOZART. And you're Squeeky-Peeky. And Stanzi-manzi. And Bini-gini! (*She surrenders.*)

CONSTANZE. Wolfi-polfi!

MOZART. Poopy-peepee! (*They giggle.*)

CONSTANZE. Now don't be stupid.

MOZART. (*Insistent: like a child.*) Come on — do it. Do it — Let's do it. 'Poppy!' (*They play a private game, gradually doing it faster, on their knees.*)

CONSTANZE. Poppy.

MOZART. (*Changing it.*) Pappy.

CONSTANZE. (*Copying.*) Pappy.

MOZART. Pappa.

CONSTANZE. Pappa.

MOZART. Pappa-pappa!

CONSTANZE. Pappa-pappa!

MOZART. Pappa-pappa-pappa-pappa!

CONSTANZE. Pappa-pappa-pappa-pappa! (*They rub*

noses.)

TOGETHER. Pappa-pappa-pappa-pappa! Pappa-pappa-pappa-pappa!

CONSTANZE. *Ah!* (*She suddenly cries out in distress, and cluthes her stomach.*)

MOZART. Stanzi! . . . Stanzi what is it? (*The VENTICELLI hurry in.*)

VENTICELLO 1. News!

VENTICELLO 2. Suddenly!

VENTICELLO 1. She's been delivered.

VENTICELLO 2. Unexpectedly.

VENTICELLO 1. Of a boy!

VENTICELLO 2. Poor little imp.

VENTICELLO 1. To be born to that couple.

VENTICELLO 2. In that room.

VENTICELLO 1. With that money.

VENTICELLO 2. And the Father a baby himself. (*During the above CONSTANZE has slowly risen, and divested herself of her stuffed apron—thereby ceasing to be pregnant. Now she turns sorrowfully and walks slowly U.S. and off it. MOZART follows her for a few steps, alarmed. He halts.*)

VENTICELLO 1. And now I hear—

VENTICELLO 2. Now I hear—

VENTICELLO 1. Something more has happened.

VENTICELLO 2. Even stranger. (*MOZART picks up a bottle—then moves swiftly into SALIERI's room.*)

MOZART. (*In panic.*) She's gone!

SALIERI. What do you mean? (*The VENTICELLI go off. MOZART moves up to SALIERI's apartment, holding his bottle, and sits on one of the gilded chairs.*)

MOZART. Stanzerl's gone away. Just for a while, she says. She's taken the baby and gone to Baden. To the spa. It will cost us the last money we have!

SALIERI. But *why?*

MOZART. She's right to go . . . It's my fault . . . She thinks I'm mad.

SALIERI. Surely not?

MOZART. Perhaps I am . . . I think I am . . . Yes . . .

SALIERI. Wolfgang . . .

MOZART. Let me tell you! Last night I saw the Figure again—the figure in my dreams . . . Only I was awake! (*Very disturbed.*) It stood before my table, all in grey, its face still grey, still masked. And this time it spoke to me! "Wolfgang Mozart—you must write now a Requiem Mass. Take up your pen and begin!"

SALIERI. A Requiem?

MOZART. I asked, "Who is this Requiem for, who has died?" It said "The work must be finished when you see me next!" Then it turned and left the room.

SALIERI. Oh, this is morbid fancy, my friend!

MOZART. It had the force of real things! . . . To tell the truth—I do not know whether it happened in my head or out of it . . . No wonder Stanzi has gone. I frightened her away . . . And now she'll miss the Vaudeville.

SALIERI. You mean it's finished? So soon?

MOZART. Oh, yes—music is easy: it's marriage that's hard!

SALIERI. I long to see it!

MOZART. Would you come, truly? The Theatre isn't grand. It's just a popular Music Hall. No one from Court will be there.

SALIERI. Do you think that matters to me? I would travel anywhere for a work by you! . . . I am no substitute for your little wife—but I know someone who could be! (*He gets up.* MOZART *rises also.*)

MOZART. Who?

SALIERI. I'll tell you what—I'll bring Katherina! She'll cheer you up!

MOZART. Katherina!

SALIERI. As I remember it, you quite enjoyed her company! (MOZART *laughs heartily.* CAVALIERI *enters, now fatter and wearing an elaborate plumed hat. She curtseys to* MOZART *and takes his arm.*)

MOZART. (*Bowing.*) Signora!

SALIERI. (*To Audience.*) And so to the opera we went — a strange band of three! (*The other two freeze.*) The First Kapellmeister — sleek as a cat. His mistress — now fat and feathered like the great songbird she'd become. And Mozart, demented and drunk on the cheap wine which was now his constant habit. (*They unfreeze.*) We went out into the suburbs — to a crowded Music Hall — in a tenement . . .

* * * *

The Theatre By The Weiden.

Two benches are brought in and placed down front. Sudden noise. A crowd of working-class Germans swarm in from the back: a chattering mass of humanity through which the three have to push their way to the front. The long table is pushed horizontally, and the rowdy audience piles on top of it, smoking pipes and chewing sausages.

Unobserved, BARON VAN SWIETEN *comes in also and stands at the back.*

MOZART. You must be indulgent now! It's my first piece of this kind! (*The three sit on the front bench:* MOZART *sick and emanciated;* CAVALIERI *blowsy and bedizened;* SALIERI *as elegant as ever.*)

SALIERI. We sat as he wished us to, among ordinary Germans! The smell of sweat and sausage was almost annihilating! (CAVALIERI *presses a mouchoir to her sensitive nose.*) (*To* MOZART.) This is so exciting!

MOZART. (*Happily.*) Do you think so?

SALIERI. (*Looking about him.*) Oh yes! This is exactly the audience we should be writing for! Not the dreary Court . . . As always — *you* show the way! (*The* AUDIENCE *freezes.*) (*To us.*) As always, he did. My pungent neighbours *rolled* on their benches at the jokes — (*They unfreeze — briefly to demonstrate this mirth.*) — And I alone in their midst heard — *The Magic Flute.* (*They freeze again. The great hymn at the end of Act 2 is heard: 'Heil sei euch Geweihten.'*) He had put the Masons into it right enough. Oh, yes — but how? He had turned them into an Order of Eternal Priests. I heard voices calling out of ancient temples. I saw a vast sun rise on a timeless land, where animals danced and children floated: and by its rays all the poisons we feed each other drawn up and burnt away! (*A great sun does indeed rise inside the Light Box, and standing in it the gigantic silhouette of a Priestly Figure extending its arms to the world in universal greeting.*) And in this sun — behold — I saw his father. No more an accusing figure, but forgiving! The Highest Priest of the Order — his hand extended to the world in love! Wolfgang feared Leopold no longer: a final Legend has been made! . . . Oh the sound — the sound of that new-found peace in him — mocking my undiminishing pain! *There* was the Magic Flute — *there beside me!* (*He points to* MOZART. *Applause from all.* MOZART *jumps up excitedly onto the bench and acknowledges the clapping with his arms flung out. He turns to us a bottle in his hand — his eyes staring: all freeze again.*) Mozart the flute, and God the relentless player. How long could the Creature stand it — so frail, so palpably mortal? And what was this I was tasting suddenly? Could it be pity? . . . *Never!*

VAN SWIETEN. (*Calling out.*) *Mozart!* (VAN SWIETEN *pushes his way to the front through the crowd of dispersing Citizens. He is outraged.*)

MOZART. (*Turning joyfully to greet him.*) Baron! You here! How wonderful of you to come!

SALIERI. (*To Audience.*) I had of course suggested it.

VAN SWIETEN. (*With cold fury.*) What have you done?

MOZART. Excellency?

VAN SWIETEN. You have put our rituals into a vulgar show!

MOZART. No, sir—

VAN SWIETEN. They are plain for all to see! And to laugh at! You have betrayed the Order.

MOZART. (*In horror.*) NO!

SALIERI. Baron, a word with you—

VAN SWIETEN. Don't speak for him, Salieri! (*To* MOZART, *with frozen contempt.*) You were ever a cruel vulgarian we hoped to mend. Stupid, hopeless task! Now you are a betrayer as well. I shall never forgive you. And depend upon it—I shall ensure that no Freemason or Person of Distinction shall assist you so long as I have life!

SALIERI. Baron, please, I must speak!

VAN SWIETEN. No, sir! Leave alone. (*To* MOZART.) I did not look for this reward, Mozart. Never speak to me. (*He goes out. The crowd disperses. The light becomes gloomy. The benches are taken off.* SALIERI, *watching* MOZART *narrowly, dismisses* KATHERINA. MOZART *stands as one dead.*)

SALIERI. Wolfgang? . . . (MOZART *shakes his head sharply—and walks away from him,* U.S., *desolate and stunned.*) Wolfgang—all is not lost. (MOZART *enters his apartment and freezes.*) (*To Audience.*) But of course it was! Now he was ruined. Broken and shunned by all men of influence. And for good measure, he did not even get his half receipts from the opera.

* * * *

(*The* VENTICELLI *come in.*)

VENTICELLO 1. Schickaneder pays him nothing.

VENTICELLO 2. Schickaneder cheats him.

VENTICELLO 1. Gives him enough for liquor.

VENTICELLO 2. And keeps all the rest.

SALIERI. I couldn't have managed it better myself. (MOZART *takes up a blanket and muffles himself in it. Then he sits at his work-table, down front, staring out at the Audience, quite still, the blanket almost over his face.*) And then silence. No word came from him at all. Why? . . . I waited each day. Nothing. . . . Why? . . . (*To the* VENTICELLI, *brusquely.*) *What does he do?* (MOZART *writes.*)

VENTICELLO 1. He sits at his window.

VENTICELLO 2. All day and all night.

VENTICELLO 1. Writing—

VENTICELLO 2. Writing—like a man possessed. (MOZART *springs to his feet, and freezes.*)

VENTICELLO 1. Springs up every moment!

VENTICELLO 2. Stares wildly at the street!

VENTICELLO 1. Expecting something—

VENTICELLO 2. Someone—

VENTICELLO 1 & VENTICELLO 2. *We can't imagine what!*

SALIERI. (*To Audience.*) *I* could! (*He also springs up excitedly, dismissing the* VENTICELLI. MOZART *and* SALIERI *now both stand staring out front.*) Who did he look for? A Figure in grey, masked and sorrowing, come to take him away. I knew what he was doing, alone in that slum! He was writing his Requiem Mass—for himself! . . . And now I confess the wickedest thing I did to him. (*His* VALET *brings him the clothes which he describes, and he puts them on, turning his back to us to don the hat—to which is attached a mask.*) My friends—there is no blasphemy a man will not commit, compelled to such a war as mine! I got me a cloak of grey. Yes, I got me a hat of grey . . . Yes . . . And a mask of grey—Yes! (*He turns round; he is masked.*) And appeared myself to the demented Creature as—*the Messenger of God!* . . . I confess that in November, 1791, I—Antonio Salieri, then as now First Royal Kapellmeister to the Empire—walked empty Vienna in the freezing moonlight for seven nights on end! That precisely as the clocks of the city struck one I would halt beneath Mozart's window—and become his more terrible clock. (*The clock strikes one.* SALIERI, *without moving from the* L. *side of the stage, raises his arms: his fingers show seven days.* MOZART *rises—fascinated and appalled—and stands equally rigidly on the* R. *side, looking out in horror.*) Every night I showed him one day less—then stalked away. Every night the face he showed me at the glass was more crazed. Finally—with no days left to him—*horror!* I arrived as usual. Halted. And instead of fingers, reached up beseechingly as the Figure of his dreams! "Come!—Come!—Come! . . . " (*He beckons to* MOZART, *insidiously.*) He stood swaying, as if he would faint off into death. But suddenly—incredibly—he realized all his little strength, and in a clear voice called down to me the words out of his opera *Don Giovanni*, inviting the statue to dinner.

MOZART. (*Pushing open the "window".*) *O statua*

gentillissimu — venite a cena! (*He beckons in his turn.*)

SALIERI. For a long moment one terrified man looked at another. Then — unbelievably — I found myself nodding, just as in the opera. Starting to move across the street! (*The rising and falling scale passage from the Overture to* Don Giovanni *sounds darkly, looped in sinister repetition. To this hollow music* SALIERI *marches slowly* U.S.) Pushing down the latch of his door — tramping up the stairs with stone feet. There was no stopping it. *I was in his dream!* (MOZART *stands terrified by his table.* SALIERI *throws open the door. An instant light change.* SALIERI *stands still, staring impassively* D.S. MOZART *addresses him urgently, and in awe.*)

MOZART. It's not finished! . . . Not nearly! . . . Forgive me. Time was I could write a Mass in a week! . . . Give me one month more, and it'll be done: I swear it! . . . He'll grant me that, surely? God can't want it unfinished! . . . Look — look, see what I've done. (*He snatches up the pages from the table and brings them eagerly to the Figure.*) Kyrie the first theme, Eleison the second, both together make a double fugue . . . (*Unwillingly* SALIERI *moves across the room — takes the pages, and sits behind the table in* MOZART's *chair, staring out front.*) Grant me time, I beg you! If you do, I swear I'll write a real piece of music. I know I've boasted I've written hundreds, but it's not true. I've written nothing finally good! (SALIERI *looks at the pages. Immediately we hear the sombre opening of the Requiem Mass. Over this* MOZART *speaks.*) Oh, it began so well. Once the world was so full, so happy! . . . All the journeys — all the carriages — all the rooms of smiles! Everyone smiled at me once — the King at Schönbrunn; the Princess at Versailles — they lit my way with candles to the clavier! — my father bowing, bowing, bowing with such joy! . . . "Chevalier Mozart, my miraculous son!" . . . Why has it all gone? . . . Why? . . . Was I so bad? So wicked? . . . Answer for Him and tell me! (*Deliberately* SALIERI *tears the paper into halves. The music stops instantly. Silence.*) (*Fearfully.*) Why? . . . Is it not good?

SALIERI. (*Stiffly.*) It is good. Yes. It is good. (*He tears off a corner of the music paper, elevates it in the manner of the Communion Service, places it on his tongue and eats it.*) (*In pain.*) I eat what God gives me. Dose after dose. For all of life. His poison. We are both poisoned, Amadeus. I with you: you with me. (*In horror* MOZART *moves slowly behind him, placing his hand over* SALIERI's *mouth—then, still from behind, slowly removes the mask and hat.* SALIERI *stares at us.*) Eccomi. Antonio Salieri. Ten years of my hate have poisoned you to death. (MOZART *falls to his knees, by the table.*)

MOZART. Oh God!

SALIERI. (*Contemptuously.*) God?! . . . God will not help you! God *does* not help!

MOZART. Oh God! . . . Oh God! . . . Oh God!

SALIERI. God does not love you, Amadeus! God does not love! He can only *use!* . . . He cares nothing for who He uses: nothing for who he denies! . . . You are no use to Him anymore—You're too weak—too sick! He has finished with you! All you can do now is *die!*

MOZART. *Ah!* (*With a groan* MOZART *crawls quickly through the trestle of the table, like an animal finding a burrow—or a child a safe place of concealment.* SALIERI *kneels by the table, calling in at his victim in desperation.*)

SALIERI. Die, Amadeus! Die, I beg you, die! . . . Leave me alone, *ti imploro!* Leave me alone at last!

Leave me alone! (*He beats on the table in his despair.*) *Alone! Alone! Alone! Alone!*

MOZART. (*Crying out at the top of his lungs.*) PA-PAAAAA! (*He freezes—his mouth open in the act of screaming—his head staring out from under the table.* SALIERI *rises in horror. Silence. Then very slowly* MO-ZART *crawls out from under the table. He stares upwards at* SALIERI. *He smiles. In a childish voice.*) Papa! (*Silence.*) Papa . . . Papa . . . (*He extends his arms upwards, imploringly. He speaks now as a very young boy.*) Take me, Papa. Take me. Put down your arms and I'll hop into them. Just as we used to do it! . . . Hop-hop-hop-hop-UP! (*He jumps up on to the table.* SALIERI *watches in horror.*) Hold me close to you, Papa. Let's sing our little Kissing Song together. Do you remember? . . . (*He sings in an infantine voice holding* SALIERI.) *Oragna figata fa! Marina gamina fa!*

SALIERI. Reduce the man: reduce the God. Behold my vow fulfilled. (*He turns* MOZART *around to face the audience.*) The profoundest voice in the world reduced to a nursery tune. (*He leaves the room, slowly, as* MOZART *resúmes his singing, taking his hat and mask.*)

MOZART. *Oragna figata fa! Marina gamina fa!* (*As* SALIERI *withdraws,* CONSTANZE *appears from the back of the stage, her bonnet in her hand. She has returned from Baden. She comes* D.S. *towards her husband, and finds him there on the table, singing in an obviously childish treble.*) *Oragna figata fa! Marina gamina fa. Fa! Fa!* (*He kisses the air, several times. Finally he becomes aware of his wife standing beside him.*) (*Uncertainly.*) Stanzi?

CONSTANZE. Wolfi? . . .

MOZART. (*In relief.*) Stanzi!

CONSTANZE. (*With great tenderness.*) Wolfi—my love! Little husband of my heart! (*He virtually falls off the table into her arms.*)

MOZART. *Oh!* (*He clings to her in overwhelming pleasure. She helps him gently to move around the table to the chair behind it, facing out front.*)

CONSTANZE. Oh, my dear one—come with me . . . Come on . . . Come on now. There . . . There . . . (MOZART *sits weakly.*)

MOZART. (*Like a child still, and most earnestly.*) Salieri . . . Salieri has killed me.

CONSTANZE. Yes, my dear. (*Practically she busies herself clearing the table of its candle, its bottle and its inkwell.*)

MOZART. He has. He told me so.

CONSTANZE. Yes, yes: I'm sure. (*She finds two pillows and places them at the left-hand head of the table.*)

MOZART. (*Petulantly.*) He did . . . He did!

CONSTANZE. Hush now, lovey. (*She helps her dying husband on to the table, now his bed. He lies down, and she covers him with her shawl.*) I'm back to take care of you. I'm sorry I went away. I'm here now, for always!

MOZART. Salieri . . . Salieri . . . Salieri . . . Salieri! (*He starts to weep.*)

CONSTANZE. Oh lovey, be silent now. No one has hurt you. You'll get better soon, I promise. Can you hear me? . . . [Lean on me] . . . If I've been a bore . . . If I've nagged a bit it's because I'm spoilt, lovey, you've spoilt me . . . (*Faintly the Lacrimosa of the Requiem Mass begins to sound.* MOZART *rises to hear it—leaning against his wife's shoulders. His hand begins feebly to beat out drum measures from the music. During the whole of the following it is evident that he is composing the Mass in his head, and does not hear his wife at all.*) You've got to get well, Wolfi—because we need you. Karl and Baby Franz as well. There's only the three of us, lovey: we don't cost much. Just don't leave us — we wouldn't know what to do without you. And you wouldn't know much either, up in Heaven, without us. You soppy thing. You can't even cut up your own meat without help! . . . I'm not clever, lovey. It can't have been easy living with a goose. But I've looked after you, you must admit that. And I've given you fun too — quite a lot really! . . . Are you listening? (*The drum strokes get slower, and stop.*) Know one thing. It was the best day of my life when you married me. And as long as I live, I'll be the most honoured woman in the world . . . Do you hear me? Can you hear me?? (*She becomes aware that* MOZART *is dead. She opens her mouth in a silent scream, raising her arm in a rigid gesture of grief. The great chord of the 'Amen' does not resolve itself, but lingers on in intense reverberation.*)

* * * *

Citizens of Vienna come in, dressed in black, from the R. CONSTANZE *kneels and freezes in grief, as Servants come in and stand at each of the four corners of the table on which the dead body lies.* VAN SWIE-TEN *also comes in.*

SALIERI. (*Hard.*) The Death Certificate said kidney failure, hastened by exposure to cold. Generous Lord Fugue paid for a pauper's funeral. Twenty other corpses. An unmarked limepit. (VAN SWIETEN *approaches* CON-STANZE.)

VAN SWIETEN. What little I can spare, you shall have for the children. There's no need to waste it on vain show. (*The Servants lift the table and bear it, with its burden,* U.C., *to the Light Box. The Citizens follow it.*)

SALIERI. What did I feel? *Relief*, of course! I confess it. And pity too, for the man I helped to destroy. I felt the pity God can never feel. I weakened God's flute to thinness. God blew—as He must—without cease. The flute split in the mouth of His insatiable need. (*The Citizens kneel. In dead silence the Servants throw* MOZART'S *body off the table into the space at the back of the stage. All depart save* SALIERI *and* CONSTANZE. *She unfreezes and starts assiduously collecting the manuscripts scattered over the floor.* SALIERI *now speaks with an increasingly ageing voice; a voice poisoned more and more by his own bitterness.*) As for Constanze, in the fullness of time she married again—a Danish diplomat as dull as a clock—and retired to Salzburg, birthplace of the Great Composer, to become the pious Keeper of his Shrine! (CONSTANZE *rises, wrapping her shawl about her, and clasping manuscripts to her bosom.*)

CONSTANZE. (*Reverentially.*) A sweeter-tongued man never lived! In ten years of blissful marriage I never heard him utter a single coarse or conceited word. The purity of his life is reflected absolutely in the purity of his music! . . . (*More briskly.*) In selling his manuscripts I charge by the ink. So many notes, so many schillings. That seems to me the simplest way. (*She leaves the stage, a pillar of rectitude.*)

SALIERI. One amazing fact emerged. Mozart did not *imagine* that masked Figure in grey who said, 'Take up your pen and write a Requiem'. It was *real!* . . . A certain bizarre nobleman called Count Walsegg had a longing to be thought a composer. He actually sent his Steward in disguise to Mozart to commission the piece—secretly, so that he could pass it off as his own work. And this he even did! After Mozart's death it was actually performed as Count Walsegg's Requiem . . . And I conducted it. (*He smiles at the Audience.*) Naturally I did. In those days I presided over all great musical occasions. (*He divests himself of his cloak.*) I even conducted the salvoes of cannon in Beethoven's dreadful *Battle Symphony*. The experience made me almost as deaf as *he* was.

* * * *

The CITIZENS *turn round and bow to him, kissing their hands extravagantly.*

And so I stayed on in the City of Musicians, reverenced by all! *On* and *on* and *on!* . . . *For thirty-two years!* . . . And slowly I understood the nature of God's punishment. (*Directly to the Audience.*) What had I asked for in that Church as a boy? Was it not Fame? Well now I had it! I was to become quite simply the most famous musician in Europe! . . . I was to be bricked up in Fame! Buried in Fame! Embalmed in Fame — but for work I knew to be absolutely worthless! . . . This was my sentence! I must endure thirty years of being called 'distinguished' — by people incapable of distinguishing! (*The* CITIZENS *have fallen on their knees to him during the proceeding, and are all clapping their hands at him silently in an adoring ring, relentlessly extending their arms upwards and upwards until they seem almost to obliterate him.*) I must smell as I wrote it the deadness of my music, whilst their eyes brimmed with tears and their throats brayed with cheering! . . . And finally — when my nose had been rubbed in Fame to vomiting — Receptions, Awards, Civic Medals and

Chains—: Suddenly His Masterstroke!—*Silence!* (*The* CITIZENS *freeze.*) It would all be taken away from me— every scrap. (*The* CITIZENS *rise, turn away from him, and walk indifferently offstage.*) Mozart's music would sound louder and louder throughout the world! And mine faded completely, till no one played it at all! I must survive to see myself become *extinct!* When they trundled me out in a carriage to get my last Award a man on the curb said "Isn't that one of the Generals from Waterloo?" (*Calling up savagely.*) *Nemico Eterno! Dio implacabile!* (*The curtains close. The wheelchair is brought on by a* SERVANT. ANOTHER *hands* SALIERI *his old dressing-gown and cap, as he divests himself of his wig and becomes once more the old man. The lights change. Six o'clock strikes. We are back in.*)

* * * *

Salieri's apartment. 1823.
The SERVANTS *leave.*

SALIERI. Dawn has come. I must release you. One moment's violence and it is over. You see, I cannot accept this. To be sucked into oblivion—not even my name remembered. Oh no. I did not live on earth to be His joke for eternity. I have one trick left me:—see how He deals with this! (*Confidently, to Audience.*) All this week I have been shouting out about murder. You heard me yourselves—do you remember? "Mozart—pieta! Pardon your Assassin! Mozart!" (*Whispers of Salieri begin: at first faintly, as at the start of the play. During the following they grow in volume, in strict and operatic counterpoint to* SALIERI'S *speeches.*)

WHISPERERS. (*Faintly.*) Salieri!

SALIERI. (*Triumphantly.*) I did this deliberately! . . .
My servants carried the news into the streets!

WHISPERERS. (*Louder.*) *Salieri!*

SALIERI. The streets repeated it to one another!

WHISPERERS. (*Louder.*) *Salieri! . . . Salieri!*

SALIERI. Now my name is on every tongue! Vienna,
City of Scandals, has a scandal worthy of it at last!

WHISPERERS. SALIERI! . . . ASSASSIN! . . . AS-
SASSIN! . . . SALIERI!

SALIERI. (*Falsetto: enjoying it.*) "Can it be true? . . .
Is it possible? . . . Did he do it after all?" . . .

WHISPERERS. (*Fortissimo.*) SALIERI!!!

SALIERI. Well, my friends, now they all will know for
sure! They will learn of my dreadful death — and they
will believe the lie forever! After today, whenever men
speak Mozart's name with love, they will speak mine
with loathing! As his name grows in the world so will
mine — *I'm going to be immortal after all!* — And He is
powerless to prevent it! . . . (*He laughs harshly.*) So,
Signore — see now if Man is mocked! (*He produces a
razor from his pocket. Then he rises, opens it, and addresses the Audience most simply, gently, and directly.*)
Amici cari. I was born a pair of ears, and nothing else.
It is only through hearing music that I know God exists.
Only through writing music that I could worship. All
around me men seek Liberty for Mankind. I sought only
slavery for myself. To be owned — ordered — exhausted
by an Absolute. Music. This was denied me — and with it
all meaning. If I cannot be Mozart then I do not wish to
be anything. Now I go to become a Ghost myself. I
will stand in the shadows when you come here to this
earth in your turns. And when you feel the dreadful bite
of your failures — and hear the taunting of unachiev-
able, uncaring God — I will whisper my name to you:
"Antonio Salieri: Patron Saint of Mediocrities!" And in

the depth of your downcastness you can pray to me. And I will forgive you. *Vi saluto.* (*He cuts his throat and falls backwards into the wheelchair. The* Cook — *who has just entered carrying a plate of buns for breakfast, screams in horror. The* Valet *rushes in at the same time from the other side. Together they pull the wheelchair, with its slumped body, backwards* u.s., *and anchor it in the* c. *The* Venticelli *appear again, in the costume of 1823.*)

Venticello 1. Beethoven's Conversation Book, November 1823. Visitors write the news for the deaf man. (*He hands a book to* Venticello 2.)

Venticello 2. (*Reading.*)'Salieri has cut his throat — but is still alive!' (Salieri *stirs and comes to life, looking about him bewilderedly. The* Valet *and the* Cook *depart. He stares out front like an astounded gargoyle.*)

Venticello 1. Beethoven's Conversation Book, 1824. Visitors write the news for the deaf man. (*He hands another book to* Venticello 2.)

Venticello 2. (*Reading.*) 'Salieri is quite deranged. He keeps claiming that he is guilty of Mozart's death, and made away with him by poison.' (*The light narrows into a bright cone, beating on* Salieri.)

Venticello 1. The German Musical Times, May 25th 1825. (*He hands a newspaper to* Venticello 2.)

Venticello 2. (*Reading.*) 'Our worthy Salieri just cannot die. In the frenzy of his imagination he is even said to accuse himself of complicity in Mozart's early death. A rambling of the mind believed in truth by no one but the deluded old man himself.' (*The music stops.* Salieri *lowers his head, conceding defeat.*)

Venticello 1. I don't believe it.

Venticello 2. I don't believe it.

Venticello 1. I don't believe it.

VENTICELLO 2. I don't believe it.

VENTICELLO 1 and VENTICELLO 2. *No one believes it in the world!* (*They go off. The light dims a little.* SALIERI *stirs—raises his head—and looks out far into the darkness of the theatre.*)

SALIERI. Mediocrities everywhere—now and to come— I absolve you all. Amen! (*He extends his arms upwards and outwards to embrace the assembled Audience in a wide gesture of Benediction—finally folding his arms high across his own breast. The light fades completely. The last four chords of the Masonic Funeral Music of* AMADEUS MOZART *sound throughout the theatre.*)

END OF PLAY

AMADEUS
AMADEUS

Working Prop List

Preset on Stage

Fortepiano
  With/ Chair (Brown)
  On Top of Fortepiano/ Salieri's Music with ribbon on
    Music Stand
  Tailor's Rule
  Candle Holder w/unlit candle
  Silver Hand Mirror
  Leather covered box of matches
  Salieri's Wig on Wig Stand (Black ribbon facing s.r.)

Wheel Chair Facing Up Stage

Small Round Brown Table
  with/ Cake Plate & Cakes (Up Stage, two edible)
    Napkin
    Small Fork

Large Wing Chair

Five Cut-Outs of Citizens in Light Box

Personal Props to Salieri

4 Large Brown Coins

OFF STAGE RIGHT

4 Brown Chairs
Throne (Gold Arm Chair with high back)

Brown Bench
Wooden Bench (Magic Flute)
Small Round Gold Table
3 Gold Chairs (One being an armchair with a low back)

1 Umbrella
1 Pillow
Rolled Paper (Commission) (Emperor)
Bell for Opera (Valet)
Bell for Salieri's door (Valet)
Large Portfolio (Constanze)
 with/ 6 loose sheets in each section, wrapped in
  shawl
Figaro Score (Mozart) (Renew Sheets each Perf.)
Plate of 'Nipples of Venus' (Cook)
Plate of Fresh Buns (Cook)
Chocolate Mug (Cook)
Venticelli I Cane
Silver Tray (Salieri's Valet)
 with/ Shaving Bowl, Soap Bowl, Razor, Hot Water
  Heater
Tall Glass w/Yogurt & Long Spoon (Forfeit Scene)
Tall Glass w/Yogurt & Long Spoon (Act II Scene 8)
2 Sausages
2 Beer Stein's
1 Long Clay Pipe
1 Short Clay Pipe
Plate of cakes (SR Gold Chair Scene)
Salieri Confession
3-tiered cake plate for Salieri Gold Scene

OFF STAGE LEFT

5 Brown Chairs
Brown Arm Chair

Pastry Table
  w/ 3-tiered Cake Plate with cakes
    3 tall glasses (Middle one with Yogurt)
    1 long spoon
    2 Cake Stands with Cakes
Tressel Table
  with/ Bottle of Red Wine
    Wooden Inkwell
    Quill Pen
    Music Sheets
    Bills
    Red Stool
    Red Chair
    Grey Blanket
Brown Bench
Wooden Bench (Magic Flute)
4 Gold Chairs

12 Scores for Venticelli
2 Umbrellas
Venticelli II Cane
Red Wine Bottle for Venticelli
Wine Glass for Venticelli
Glass of White Wine (Strack)
Winding Sheet
2 Beethoven Conversation Books (Venticelli I)
German Musical Times (Venticelli I)
"Seraglio" Score (Mozart)
Tapper (Salieri's Valet)
Matches
Silver Tray with 4 White & Gold Cups & Saucers
  w/Coffee (Valet: M. Nelson)
Sheet of Music (Katherina Cavalieri)
1 Pillow

Towel for Salieri's Valet
1 Magic Flute Beer Mug
2 Pieces of Sausage
1 Long Pipe

UP STAGE

Mattress

Notes:
Gold Throne must move to s.l. during Intermission
Brown Arm Chair moves from s.l. to s.r. after
   "Seraglio"

Amadeus Costume Plot

SALIERI

Heavy Tapestry Robe
Shawl
Noile Cap
Blue 18C Coat
Tan Moire Vest
Blue Breeches
Cream Tights
Black Shoes
2 18C Shirts w/Jabots
2 18C Dickies w/Cuffs
Handkerchief
Wig Bag and Bow
Gold 18C Coat
Cream Breeches
Brown 18C Topcoat
Brown Felt Tricorn
Grey Spectre Robe
Grey Tricorn w/Attached Mask
Mason's Apron
Gloves

MOZART

Pea Green Brocade 18C Coat
Cream Moire Vest
Cream Breeches
18C Dickies and Cuffs
Two 18C shirts with Jabots
Six Pair Cream Tights (Three Pair Darker)
Three Pair 18C Shoes: Cream, Black, Brown
Wig Bag and Bows

Black Chapeau de Bras
Melon Pink Brocade 18C Coat
Cerisse Brocade 18C Coat
Lavendar 18C Coat
Rust Brocade 18C Coat
Cream Brocade Vest
Maroon Corduroy 18C Coat.
Tan/White Striped Vest
Brown Ottoman Breeches
Gold 18C Coat
Brown Wool 18C Coat
Black Wool 18C Topcoat
Black Felt Tricorn
Handkerchief
Sword
Black Knitted Gloves

CONSTANZE

Cream 18C Dress, Two Pieces
Flowered Petticoat
Paniers
Melon Overskirt and Bodice
Lace Cap
Changeable Silk Dress, Two Pieces
Mask
Cream Stockings
Garters
Brown Silk Pelisse
Brown Straw and Silk Hat
Lace Shawl
Brown Tweed Dress
Paisley Shawl
Brown Straw and Wool Hat
Silk Noile Apron and Pregnancy pad

Pearl Earrings
Pearl Necklace
Pantaloons
Cream Shoes
Brown Shoes
Tan Petticoat with Hip Rolls

VENTICELLO I

Blue Grey 19C Topcoat
Blue Maroon Plaid Trousers
Black Shoes
Gloves
Blue Grey Tophat
Two 19C Dickeys with Black Stock
Blue Velvet Brocade 18C Coat
Blue Fialle Vest
Blue Velvet Breeches
Cream Tights
Wig Bag and Bow
Blue Grey 18C Topcoat
Blue Grey Tricorn
Two 18C Dickeys and Cuffs

VENTICELLO II

Brown 19C Topcoat
Brown Plaid Trousers
Black Shoes
Gloves
Brown Tophat
Two 19C Dickeys with Black Stock
Brown Velvet Brocade 18C Coat
Brown Fialle Vest

Brown Velvet Breeches
Cream Tights
Wig Bag and Bow
Brown 18C Topcoat
Brown Tricorn
Two 18C Dickeys and Cuffs

EMPEROR JOSEPH II

Cream with Gold Brocade Coat
Gold Brocade Vest
Yellow Breeches
Cream Tights
Black Shoes
Order Sash
Jeweled Star
18C Dickies and Cuffs
Wig bag and Bow
Handkerchief
Sword
18C Coat, Distressed
Cape
Distressed Tricorn

VAN SWIETEN

Brown Moire 18C Coat
Tan Brocade Vest
Brown Ottoman Breeches
Two 18C Dickies and cuffs
Cream Tights
Black Shoes
Brown 18C Topcoat
Brown Felt Tricorn

Gloves, Black Leather
Mason's Apron
Wig Bag and Bow

ORSINI-ROSENBERG

Yellow-Green 18C Coat
Ribbon Striped Vest
Green Velvet Breeches
Cream Tights
Black Shoes
18C Dickies and Cuffs
Sword
Chapeau de Bras
Distressed Tricorn
Cape

VON STRACK

Taupe Velvet 18C Coat
Brocade Flowered Vest
Brown Taupe Fialle Breeches
Cream Tights
Black Shoes
18C Dickies and cuffs
Sword
Chapeau de Bras
Distressed Tricorn
Cape, Scarf

BONNO

Tiered Topcoat
Black Brocade Vest
Two White Dickeys with Black Stock

Black Trousers
Black Tophat
Black Gloves
Black Breeches
Black Velvet Vest
Grey Coat, Velvet
Two 18C Dickies with Cuffs
Black Tights
Dark Rust Coat
Black 18C Topcoat
Black Tricorn
White Tights

CITIZEN/ GENTLEMAN AT FIGARO/GHOST FATHER FIGURE

Top Coat
Top Hat
Two White Dickeys with Black Stock
Grey Trousers
Black Shoes
Black Gloves
Green 18C Coat
Brocade Vest
Green Velvet Breeches
Black Tricorn
Two 18C Dickies with Cuffs
White Tights
Black Cape
Brown Vest

PRIEST

19C Topcoat
Black Tophat

Two White Dickeys with Black Stock
Grey Trousers
Black Shoes
Black Gloves, Wool
Grey Breeches
Green Satin Vest
Green Brocade Coat
Black Tricorn
Two 18C Dickies with Cuffs
18C Topcoat
Priest's Cassock
Silver Dickie
Black Skull Cap

CITIZEN

Gold Breeches
18C Vest
Two 18C Dickies with Cuffs
Black Tricorn
Teal Velvet Coat
Black Shoes
Black Gloves
19C Topcoat
Black Tophat
Two White Dickeys with Stock
Black Trousers
Brown 18C Topcoat
Brown Tricorn

MAJOR DOMO

19C Topcoat
Black Tophat

White Dickey with Black Stock
Black Vest
Black Pants
Black Gloves
Grey Velvet Coat
Black Vest With Silver Braid
Black Breeches
Two 18C Dickies and Cuffs
Black Tights
Domo Pants
Plain Black Vest
Blue/Brown Tweed Coat
Brown Cape
Brown Tricorn
Domo Pants
Domo Vest
White Tights
18C Topcoat
Tricorn
Black Gloves
Domo Costume
White Stockings

COOK

19C Topcoat with Fur
Gaiters
Gloves
Black Shoes
Grey Breeches
Striped Nightshirt
Apron
Brown Cotton Robe
Chef Hat

18C Striped Shirt
Beige Stockings
Blue 18C Coat
Black Vest
Faded Grey 18C Coat

VALET, SALIERI'S

19C Topcoat
Tophat
Leather Gaiters
Black Gloves, Aged Wool
Black Shoes
Brown Breeches
Beige Tights
Cheesecloth Shirt
Green Vest with Sleeves
Two Jabot
Green Cotton Bathrobe
Grey Breeches
Pale Green Brocade Vest
Brocade Coat
Two Cuffs and Dickies
Valet Breeches
Green Vest
Brown Tweed Coat
Brown Tricorn

CITIZEN/CATHERINA

Black Cape
Black Bodice

Black Skirt
Black Petticoat
Black Bonnet
Black Gloves
Brown Shoes
Black Silk Dress
Black Shawl
Lavendar Bodice and Underskirt
Gold/Beige Robe
Ostrich Feather Ornament
Fat Pad
Lavendar Horsehair Hat
Gold/Grey Overdress
Single Strand Pearl Necklace
Double Strand Pearl Necklace
Pearl Earrings
Cream Shoes
Cream Tights
Paniers
Petticoat

FRAU SALIERI

Paniers
Petticoat
Gold Brocade Dress
Black Shoes
Cream Tights
Necklace/Earrings, Pearl
Black 18C Dress
Shawl
Black Petticoat
Black Dress, Cape, Bonnet Gloves

CITIZEN, FEMALE

Salmon Silk Dress
Paniers
Petticoat
Pearl Necklace, Earrings
Black Shoes
Black Silk Dress
Shawl
Grey Dress
Grey Cape
Grey Bonnet
Black Petticoat
Grey Gloves

VALETS (SIX)

Blue Coats
White Vests
Blue Pants
Wig Bags and Bows
Cream Tights
Black Shoes
Two 18C Dickies and Cuffs each
18C Topcoat, Black Tricorn (For one VALET)

R.P. Screen
PRATER
THEATRE PEOPLE
PALACE
THEATRE BOXES
SALIERI GOLD
LIBRARY

Set design: AMADEUS.

131

SALIERI'S MARCH as played by both Salieri and Mozart, Mozart playing it faster, lighter, and less decoratively.

MOZART'S TRANSFORMATION PROCESS:

"That fourth doesn't quite work, does it?"

"Let's try the third above . . . . "

"Ah! . . .

p slow

132

"NON PIU ANDRAI" arranged for piano by Kevin Leeman

At first tentatively

THE DRESSER

(LITTLE THEATRE—DRAMA)

By RONALD HARWOOD

10 men, 3 women—Complete interior

Sir, the last of the great, but dying, breed of English actor/managers, is in a very bad way tonight. As his dresser tries valiantly to prepare him to go on stage as King Lear, Sir is having great difficulty remembering who and where he is, let alone Lear's lines. With a Herculean effort on the part of Norman, the dresser, Sir finally does make it on stage, and through the performance—no thanks to the bombs of the *Luftwaffe*, which are falling all around the theatre (the play takes place back stage on an English provincial theatre during an air raid during World War II). It is to be Sir's last performance, though; for backstage in his dressing room after the performance, the worn out old trouper dies—leaving his company—and, in particular, his loyal dresser—alone with their loneliness. "A stirring evening . . . burns with a love of the theater that conquers all . . . perfectly observed, devilishly entertaining backstage lore."—N.Y. Times. "Sheer wonderful theatricality . . . I think you'll love it as much as I did."— N.Y. Daily News. "Enthralling, funny and touching. Lovingly delineated dramatic portraits . . . Almost any actor would jump at them."—N.Y. Post. "A wonderfully affectionate and intelligent play about the theatre."—The Guardian, London.

EQUUS

(LITTLE THEATRE—DRAMA)

By PETER SHAFFER

5 men, 4 women, 6 actors to play horses—Basic setting

Martin Dysart, a psychiatrist, is confronted with Alan Strang, a boy who has blinded six horses. To the owner of the horses the horror is simple: he was unlucky enough to employ 'a loony'. To the boy's parents it is a hideous mystery: Alan had always adored horses, and although Dora Strang may have been a slightly overindulgent mother and Frank Strang a slightly tetchy father, they both loved their son. To Dysart it is a psychological puzzle to be untangled and pain to be alleviated . . . or rather, given his profession, that is what it ought to be. As it turns out, it is something far more complex and disturbing: a confrontation with himself as well as with Alan, in which he comes to an inescapable view of man's need to worship and the distortions forced on that need by "civilized" society. Since this is a story of discovery, the reader's excitement would be diminished by a detailed account of its development. "The closest I have seen a contemporary play come to reanimating the spirit of mystery that makes the stage a place of breathless discovery rather than a classroom for rational demonstration. Mr. Shaffer may have been trying for just such iconography—a portrait of the drives that lead men to crucify themselves—there. Here I think he's found it."—Walter Kerr, N.Y. Times.

Other Publications for Your Interest

WHITE LIARS
(COMEDY)

By PETER SHAFFER

2 men, 1 woman—Interior

Produced in London and on Broadway as a companion piece to *Black Comedy*. It featured Geraldine Page as a fortune-teller to whom a youth comes with his "buddy" in tow. He doesn't want his fortune told, but he wants to pretend it's been told. What he really wants is to bribe the fortune-teller to frighten his "buddy" so he will relinquish his girl to him. But the "Buddy" sees through the ruse—all the false biography he had planted with the other fellow comes back through the fortune-teller; and both he and the fortune-teller make a discovery about love. "A deft, sharply etched study of three characters."—N.Y. Daily News.

THE PRIVATE EAR AND THE PUBLIC EYE
(LITTLE THEATRE—COMEDY)

By PETER SHAFFER

2 men, 1 woman

Unanimous critical acclaim greeted both the London and Broadway productions of this brace of delightful plays. The first, **The Private Ear**, is a rueful romance in which a boy makes a date with a girl he met at a concert, and has his worldly friend coach him for the occasion. Not only is the coaching all wrong for the occasion, but the girl turns out to be a very rude disappointment. In **The Public Eye** we meet a snappy private detective who dresses like an unmistakable neon sign and is constantly eating yogurt and grapefruit. He has been hired to tail an accountant's wife, but has succeeded in giving himself away every time. "The twin comedies are delightful any way you want to look at them. . . . They are deftly contrived, cheerfuly entertaining."—N.Y. Herald Tribune. "They are silky-smooth, literate, witty and irresistibly human."—N.Y. Daily News. "They have in common a most winning quality of humor, sympathy, fresh characterization, imaginative observation and brightly artful entertainment."—N.Y. Post. "At the conclusion of each you know that you have been a guest at two lucid moments of truth."—N.Y. World-Telegram & Sun.

Other Publications for Your Interest

THE ROYAL HUNT OF THE SUN
(ALL GROUPS—HISTORY)
By PETER SHAFFER

22 men, 2 women—Cyc, drops, inset

The expedition of the Spanish under Pizzaro to the land of the Incas told in dazzling spectacle and moral chiaroscuro. After general absolution for any crimes they may commit against the pagan Incas, the conquerors set forth upon the sea. The Inca god is a sun god, ruler of the riches and people of Peru, and thought to be immortal. But the Spaniards have come in conquest rather than in reverence. There is a misunderstanding, confusion, and a slaughter in which the Spaniards kill 3000 unarmed and take the sun god captive. The ransom is 9000 pounds of gold. The avaricious Spaniards mutiny, try the sun god in kangaroo court, and then garrot him. He does not revive, and the Incas behold their dead god. "High intelligence and bold, imaginative reach . . . It has elements of the masque (and) pageant, soaring passages that recall the stage to its lofty enterprise, and a theme of enduring significance."—N.Y. Times. "Greatest play of our generation."—London Daily Mail.

BLACK COMEDY
(LITTLE THEATRE—FARCE)
By PETER SHAFFER

5 men, 3 women—Interior

Taking a page from the Chinese theatre, this farce opens on a dark stage (which is light to the characters), then blows a fuse throwing them all in the dark (which is light to the audience), and ends with lights reconnected (i.e., with a dark stage). What we see in the "dark" is this: A girl bringing her wealthy father to meet her fiance, an improvident sculptor, and to impress him, the sculptor has both invited a wealthy art patron and stolen the fine furniture from the apartment next door for his bare pad. Not only have the lights gone out, but everything else turns cockeyed—the neighbor returns too soon, the art patron is mistaken for an electrician, and a former flame pixies the proceedings from the bedroom. "Grand slapstick . . . Jolted me with laughter, and I was sorry indeed when the stage went dark and farce ended."—N.Y. Daily News. "A remarkably ingenious farce."—Wall Street Journal. "A truly hilarious and original farce . . . farcical situations and amusing characters that keep the hilarity spinning festively in the air."—N.Y. Post. "An evening with this uproarious play is like the rediscovery of laughter."—N.Y. World Journal Tribune. One of the biggest hits of the season and a perfect play for Little Theatre and College groups.